D0875933

Illustrated Handbook of

GYMNASTICS,

TUMBLING,

and TRAMPOLINING

ILLUSTRATED HANDBOOK OF GYMNASTICS, TUMBLING, AND TRAMPOLINING

William T. Boone

Parker Publishing Company, Inc.

West Nyack, New York

WILLIAM WOODS COLLEGE LIBRARY

©1976, *by*

PARKER PUBLISHING COMPANY, INC.

West Nyack, N.Y.

*All rights reserved. No part of this book
may be reproduced in any form or by any
means, without permission in writing
from the publisher.*

Library of Congress Cataloging in Publication Data

Boone, William T.
    Illustrated handbook of gymnastics, tumbling, and
trampolining.

    Bibliography: p.
    Includes index.
    1. Gymnastics. 2. Tumbling. 3. Trampoline.
I. Title.
GV511.B66   796.4'1   75-25964
ISBN 0-13-451203-0

Printed in the United States of America

GV
511
B66

To my wife BRENDA,
son TOBY, and daughter TARA

59022

What's In This Book for You

In recent years, the sport of gymnastics has grown enormously as a result of greater exposure to the American people. In addition, gymnastics is a sport that requires considerable discipline and courage and thus warrants the appreciation and respect of the spectators. However, despite the growing concern for gymnastics, there is still the need to help the gymnastics coach cope more effectively with the coaching and teaching of gymnastics.

Part I is devoted to gymnastic skills. It is hoped that the sequential presentation of the skills will enhance skill acquisition and routine formation. Although certain skills have been deleted from the text, the author feels that a sufficient number of skills and routines have been included to do a quality job of teaching and/or coaching at either the secondary or college level.

Guides for judging gymnastic performance are analyzed in Part II of the text. An understanding of these guides is definitely a positive step to increase the number of qualified coaches in the sport of gymnastics.

Part III is devoted to the science of injury prevention, and the treatment of gymnastic injuries. Although physical injuries may occur regardless of the preventive measures designed to control this aspect of coaching, it is the responsibility of both the coach and the gymnast to assist each other in an effort to prevent potentially unsafe events from transpiring.

Part IV is unique in that it presents an application of basic biomechanics and kinesiology to selected gymnastic skills. The coach will gain a more intense appreciation for the biomechanics of successful coaching as opposed to the traditional trial and error approach. The fact of the matter is that the trial and error approach may be rewarding, provided correct biomechanics are applied. However, the concerned leader will take the information contained in this section to bridge the gap between the average and the excellent gymnastics coach.

Finally, the author stresses the importance of knowing why movement occurs, based on the principles of biomechanics. Thus, it is felt that a logical approach to the study of gymnastics is presented. In addition, it is hoped that the coach reading this handbook will come to share the enthusiasm and rewards the author has gained from the teaching and coaching of gymnastics.

Although the handbook is a combination of four parts, each part may be viewed separately, just as one learns first a skill and then second a routine. Also, the illustration of the intermediate and advanced skills should provide additional insight into the coaching and teaching of individual and sequence skills.

William T. Boone

CONTENTS

2—FLOOR EXERCISE *(cont.)*

> *Third Sequence–Run, Front Handspring, Pike Front Salto, Front Hand-spring, Swedish Fall, Neck Spring One-Half Turn to Front Sup-port*
>
> *Fourth Sequence–Run, Diving Forward Roll, Headspring to Knees, Press-Kick to Handstand, Pirouette, Snap Down from Handstand*
>
> *Fifth Sequence–Run, Round-Off Back Handspring, Full-Twisting Back Salto to Stand*

> *Training for Side Horse*
> *Side Horse Skills*
> > *Front Support*
> > *Rear Support*
> > *Feint Support*
> > *Alternate Leg Cuts*
> > *Single Leg Circle*
> > *Single Leg Stockli Mount*
> > *Loop, Double Leg Circles, Moore Without Pommels*
> > *Loop, Uphill Travel, Circle, Downhill Travel, Loop*
> > *Circle, Moore Without Pommels, Circle, Loop, Back Kehre-In*
> > *Circles, Moore, Immediate Moore, Circle, Break into Reverse Scissors*
> > *Front Scissors, Circle, Downhill Travel, Loop*
> > *Loop, Immediate Circle Without Pommels, Moore Without Pommels, Loop to Front Vault Dismount*

> *Training for Vaulting*
> > *Run*
> > *Hurdle*
> > *Takeoff*
> > *Preflight*
> > *Push-off*
> > *Afterflight*
> > *Landing*
> *Vaulting Skills*
> > *Squat (on Side Horse)*
> > *Flank (on Side Horse)*
> > *Front (on Side Horse)*
> > *Rear (on Side Horse)*
> > *Straddle (on Side Horse)*
> > *Straddle (Long Horse, Far End Valt)*
> > *Squat (Long Horse, Far End Vault)*
> > *Stoop (Long Horse, Far End Vault)*
> > *Front Handspring*
> > *Hecht*
> > *Hecht (Full Twist)*

11—CARE AND TREATMENT OF GYMNASTIC INJURIES (*cont.*)

Contents

13—APPLICATION OF MECHANICAL LAWS AND PRINCIPLES TO GYMNASTICS *(cont.)*

PART I

Illustrated Gymnastics, Tumbling, and Trampolining

This section was written primarily for coaches and gymnasts interested in basic, intermediate, and advanced gymnastics. The purpose of this section is to provide training and coaching hints for GYMNASTICS (Chapter 2–Floor Exercise, Chapter 3–Side Horse, Chapter 4–Vaulting, Chapter 5–Parallel Bars, Chapter 6–Horizontal Bar, and Chapter 7–Rings), TUMBLING (Chapter 1), and TRAMPOLINE (Chapter 8). To facilitate an understanding of the coaching hints, the author has provided numerous illustrations that may be considered unique or seldom found in most gymnastic books.

1

Tumbling

Tumbling is often referred to as the foundation of gymnastics. In fact, all gymnasts should be encouraged to learn as many tumbling skills as possible to enhance psychophysiological factors such as: (1) strength; (2) endurance; (3) flexibility; (4) coordination; (5) kinesthetic perception; (6) courage; and (7) self-confidence.

Coaches often feel that the acquisition of apparatus skills will be easier if a gymnast first learns tumbling skills. However, to what extent tumbling skills can actually be transferred to other areas of gymnastics is still unclear. The learning and execution of a great majority of skills are highly specific and not necessarily related. There are many instances where gymnasts have learned advanced parallel bar or ring routines without direct exposure to tumbling. Nevertheless, it would seem appropriate and logical to relate the similarities between a tumbling skill and an apparatus skill.

TRAINING FOR TUMBLING

Tumbling is often used as a method of warming up for all members of a team. In fact, some mild tumbling should probably precede more vigorous stretching exercises—the point being that some tumbling would elevate the body temperature, a factor conducive to developing flexibility.

It is of the utmost importance that the tumbling skills be learned and practiced in an organized and progressive manner, starting with forward rolls and followed gradually by more difficult skills (e.g., front salto). All gymnasts should participate and tumble together. They should also learn how to spot each other and gradually assume more responsibility for both their participation and safety.

Either the coach or a gymnast assuming such responsibility should direct and supervise training exercises for tumbling. These exercises are critically important and helpful to a concerned gymnast. They are designed to develop strong and flexible legs, flexible shoulders and lower back, strong arms and upper back, and strong abdominal and hip flexor muscles.

To increase the strength of the legs, gymnasts should engage in vertical jumps with the legs straight, tucked, and straddled. Practicing these exercises several times daily will not only maintain good muscle tone, but will also increase the strength and power of the quadriceps, hamstrings, gluteal, and calf muscles.

The shoulder region and the lower back are made more flexible by engaging in a bridge-up or backbend. This is a common warm-up exercise, but it is seldom executed correctly. Too often gymnasts fail to fully extend the arms, keep the feet flat on the floor (mat), and position the shoulders over the hands. These types of problems must be corrected. An interesting and rewarding variation is to keep the legs together and straight as the shoulders are moved over the hands.

The legs (hamstrings) and the lower back are stretched and become more flexible as a gymnast leans or stretches forward in the straddle position. The stretch should be over one leg (right or left), the next leg, and finally in the middle. Do not allow bouncing. The stretch should be slow and held for some five to ten seconds. The back should be as straight as possible. Allowing the back to bend defeats the objective of the exercise. It is advisable to use a partner to position the body to attain the desired benefit, as well as to avoid muscle and ligamentous soreness from unintentional bouncing. Moreover, by working on splits to both sides, the musculature of the legs, thighs, and hips will be stretched. Again, a partner can be helpful in controlling the degree of stretch. For example, an interesting variation is to hold on to an apparatus (bars, beam, or side horse) while the partner raises a leg to the desired position.

Gymnasts are going to develop arm and upper back strength and endurance from simply engaging in apparatus work. However, to insure an increase in strength potential, it is often necessary to engage in dips on the parallel bars, chins on the high bar, handstand push-ups on the floor, or simply push-ups on the floor.

The abdominal and hip flexor muscles are strengthened by engaging in bent-knee sit-ups. To some extent, straight-leg sit-ups will tend to strengthen the hip flexors (iliopsoas) more than the abdominal muscles. Such an exercise may also predispose young gymnasts to lower back problems, such as an increased anterior convexity of the lumbar spine (lordosis). The bent-knee sit-up takes the strain off the lower back and places greater tension on the abdominal muscles.

TUMBLING SKILLS

Forward Roll

The forward roll is often the first skill taught to beginners, yet it is used with various combinations during floor exercise and has similar features with respect to e.g., the front salto on the floor or, perhaps, on the parallel bars by the advanced gymnast. Hence, its importance and correct mechanics should not be overlooked.

Too often the beginner is instructed to place his hands on the mat while assuming a squatting position and then "tuck up tight" as the feet exert force against the mat. Unfortunately, this technique is rather difficult since the beginner has very limited control over his angular motion. Hay (1973) compares this technique with tumbling skills such as the front or back flips. That is, once airborne, the only way of increasing the rotational speed is by shortening the radius of rotation (and thus, the term "tuck up tight").

It thus seems reasonable to teach the forward roll according to the following steps:

1. Initiate the forward displacement of the center of gravity outside of the base by leaning forward from a semi-tuck position.

2. As the hands contact the mat, the arms should bend as the chin is placed close to the chest to allow the back of the shoulders to touch the mat. Actually the arms should be fairly extended and then quickly flexed upon contacting the mat. The extensor muscles (triceps) of the arms contract eccentrically to dissipate the force of impact.

3. At the instant of shoulder contact, the legs should be extended for two reasons: (1) The muscular force derived from straightening the legs is directed backward and downward against the mat, of which the counterforce of the mat pushes back and propels the performer; and (2) the rotation of the roll can be effectively controlled by the legs especially when straight. For example, to speed up the rotation, the forward and downward movement of the legs (hip extension) acquires considerable angular momentum that is transferred to the rest of the body. This additional angular momentum supplements the forces realized before the feet left the mat.

4. The roll is completed by throwing the arms forward of the base to aid in moving the center of gravity over the feet. It is not necessary to grasp the shins to attain a tighter tuck when there is insufficient angular momentum to complete the roll to the feet. Instead, as the hips move closer to the mat, the hips and knees should flex (bringing the feet close to the buttocks) as the arms are thrown forward to contribute momentum to the total body (Boone, 1974c).

Backward Roll

Although the backward roll is generally taught from a squatting position, from which the performer then pushes backward to displace the line of gravity outside of the base (the feet), the resulting backward angular momentum is often insufficient to overcome the resistance met when the hands contact the mat. Hence, for the individual who knows how to place the hands, and the importance of a tight tuck, he may benefit greatly by starting the backward roll from a standing position. This technique allows the force of gravity to begin the movement, thereby minimizing the resistance to the backward rotary motion (Jensen, 1970).

It is important that each consecutive motion contributes maximally to be effective. That is, there should be no pause or hesitation between the flexion of the hips and knees (during the descent) and the thrust of the upper body backward. Otherwise, the advantage gained by allowing gravity to begin the movement is neutralized.

Like the use of the legs in the front roll, the backward thrust of the upper body (in the back roll) enhances the angular momentum of the legs as they move up and over the base. As the feet contact the mat to establish a new base, the center of gravity is moved within it as the body is straightened.

Cartwheel

It is important to begin this skill with the arms extended above the shoulders and the body facing the direction in which the cartwheel is to be performed. The initial movement of the left foot forward (for a left hand placement first) serves as the push-off foot to continue the forward movement of the center of gravity outside of the body (dynamic balance). As the hands move toward the floor (aided by hip flexion), the rear leg moves upward as the push with the front foot completes the transition from the standing position to the inverted handstand position with the legs spread. Hence, the front foot creates the necessary angular momentum to invert the body. The swing of the rear leg can assist depending upon the force of the lift, such as when performing a side aerial.

The head should be back so as to see the mat, which is a very important part of the execution. Also, by pushing against the mat with each hand, additional angular momentum is realized to continue the movement of the center of gravity beyond the hands and eventually over a new base with the chest facing the direction of performance (rather than a side-facing astride position).

Back Walkover

The performer stands facing the opposite direction in which he intends to move. The right foot, e.g., is placed forward of what becomes the push (or rear) foot. The arms should be raised above the shoulders before leaning backward. As the head moves backward to see the floor, the hands should be placed on the mat with the arms fully stretched. As the hands are making contact, the right leg moves quickly up and back to aid in moving the center of gravity closer to the base. The push leg serves to accomplish the same purpose.

At the time of the push, the shoulders should be above the hands. As the hips move over the base, the legs are spread to lessen the weight directed above the hands. Also, the continued up and back movement of the lift leg aids in moving the center of gravity from outside the base to over the base and eventually out again. As the right foot contacts the mat, the arms push against the mat to impart additional angular momentum to position the performer on his feet (Boone, 1974b).

Front Walkover

A front walkover is, in essence, merely the reverse of a back walkover. Starting from a standing position, the gymnast leans forward to place the hands on the mat. This movement, which moves the line of gravity outside the base, is accompanied by a push with the front foot and an up and forward movement of the rear leg. As the hips move above the base, the eyes should focus on the mat to keep an arch in the back. As the foot contacts the mat, a push by the arms will help in raising the upper body to a position above the base. However, it is more important to be flexible than strong.

Round-Off Back Handspring

The round-off is used to convert linear momentum into either backward momentum (back handspring) or vertical motion (back salto which may combine both vertical and backward forces). (See Figure 1-1.) Hence, a poor round-off often

Figure 1-1: Round-Off Back Handspring.

distracts from the conversion process resulting in a less than desired execution of subsequent skills.

Likewise, the execution of the back handspring can either serve as an effective impetus to the back salto or reduce any chance of successfully completing the back salto. The main coaching hints to hasten the desired execution are:

1. The hurdle must be diagonal and not vertical. Too much of a vertical component will result in a loss of some of the linear momentum gained from the run.

2. The one-half turn of the body must be completed in the inverted position so that the descent of the legs is maximum. If the turn is not completed, then the force derived from hip flexion is reduced upon contacting the mat.

3. From the inverted position, the legs descend together to achieve additive forces.

4. There is a continuous and forceful back-upward thrust of the arms, head, and chest. The angular momentum derived from the arms is transferred to the body as they begin to slow down.

5. The feet push against the floor as the body becomes unstable. The extension at the hip, knee, and ankle joints moves the center of gravity further from the base as well as increasing angular momentum.

6. As the hands contact the mat, the shoulders should remain extended, provided the angular momentum is suffcient to allow the body to pass through a handstand position. Once again, the arms are thrown back-upward to move into the next skill, e.g., a back flip.

Back Salto

Provided the body retains some of the angular momentum derived, for example, from a round-off back handspring, then the performer can think more about obtaining the desired height for optimum execution. However, the basic mechanics include a vigorous back-upward thrust of the arms, head, and upper body to generate the necessary backward spin to get over and a tight tuck to reduce the resistance to the rotary motion. It is important that a performer look first and then tuck, otherwise the rotary speed will be insufficient to rotate to the feet.

When a back salto is preceded by a round-off or a round-off back handspring, it is important to realize that all forces should be applied sequentially. Timing and proper direction of all available forces will minimize extraneous body actions, which are often directed away from the intended line of motion.

In explosive events such as tumbling and floor exercise, the coach must be able to respond very quickly when analyzing skills without the aid of film. For example, by knowing the height of a back flip (c. of g.) from the floor (5 feet), one can then calculate the time taken in the fall by the following formula (Rasch and Burke, 1967):

$$t = \sqrt{\frac{5}{\frac{1}{2}g}} = \sqrt{.311} = .56 \text{ sec.}$$

One can quickly see that a coach doesn't have much time to analyze a skill. Moreover, if he is only 1 second away from the performer, he will not be an effective spotter since the gymnast falls from the top of the flip to the floor in only .56 seconds.

Double Back Salto

Figure 1-1a: Double Back Salto.

The double back salto has become a frequent introductory movement for floor exercise routines. (See Figure 1-1a). Obviously, it must be learned in a tumbling series prior to its combination with floor exercise skills. The main coaching hints are:

1. The round-off back handspring must be performed with ease.
2. The gymnast must first be able to execute a back salto with considerable height. Moreover, the takeoff must be nearly as vertical as possible.
3. The movement of the arms must be vertical and then backward.
4. It is very important that the tuck is tight and complete throughout the skill. The second salto is usually tighter than the first salto.
5. Both flips should be completed at about the same distance from the mat, i.e., both flips are not performed while going up or down but rather one execution occurs during the ascent and the second during the descent.
6. Upon landing, the performer's arms should once again assume the over-head positon.

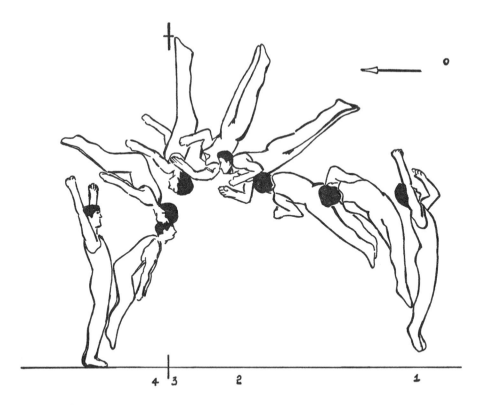

Figure 1-1b: Back Salto, Full Twist.

Back Salto, Full Twist

Generally, a tumbler will learn a salto first from a tuck, then a pike, and finally a layout position. Upon mastering the layout back salto, he can then begin to learn the full-twisting back salto. (See Figure 1-1b.) The main coaching hints are:

1. The takeoff must be as vertical as possible.

2. The feet must reach a position slightly above (horizontal) the head and chest. At this point, one-half of the twist should be completed. That is, the performer should be able to see the floor.

3. From the aforementioned horizontal position to the inverted position, the performer must complete the final one-half twist. Hence, the full twist is completed in the first 90 degrees of the entire movement.

4. The second 90 degrees are used for the descent, which is usually evident by a slight hip flexion and cervical hyperextension.

5. The floor should be visible throughout the skill. Upon contacting the floor, the arms should be raised to a forward-upward position.

6. The movement of the arms into the body enhances the twisting action, whereas extending the arms during the descent stops the twist (Boone, 1974a).

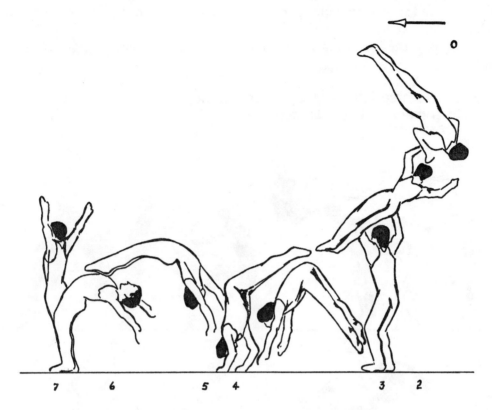

Figure 1-1c: Back Salto, One and One-Half Twists.

Back Salto, One and One-Half Twists, Front Headspring

The one and one-half twists back salto is simply a one-half twist continuation of the full-twisting back salto. This is an excellent skill for continuing forward motion. (See Figure 1-1c.) The main coaching hints are:

1. The full twist part of the one and one-half twists must be completed at the inverted (vertical) position.

2. The remaining one-half twist is completed during the descent phase (remaining 90 degrees of the 180 degree arc from takeoff to landing).

3. The arms should be extended above the shoulders as the feet contact the mat. Prior to this phase, however, the arms must be tightly wrapped around the body.

4. The hands lead the forward motion of the body. They are placed on the mat in a bent-arm position. The forehead should accompany the placement of the hands.

5. As the hips acquire a pike and move beyond the points of support, the legs must be forcefully extended vertically (transfer of momentum). At the same time, the arms are extended too (action-reaction).

6. The head should remain hyperextended to maintain the desired curvature of the back (lumbar hyperextension).

7. Finally, as the feet contact the mat, the arms should remain in the overhead position.

Front Salto (Reverse Lift) Step-Out, Handspring, Front Salto (American Lift), Headspring

Figure 1-2:   Reverse Lift Front Salto (Step Out), Handspring, American Lift Front Salto, Headspring.

The reverse lift and the traditional arm lift front saltos are compared and mechanically analyzed in Chapter 13. In this case, the reverse lift method is used during the first front salto (with a step-out into an immediate handspring). The second front salto is actually a continuation of the handspring. The technique used is the American lift followed by a headspring to a static position. (See Figure 1-2.) The main coaching hints are:

1. Most importantly, the takeoff must be as vertical as possible.

2. The arms must travel to the back and upward, to aid in lifting the body vertically. Once again, the principle of transfer of momentum is evident.

3. The tuck should be tight, although it is generally not as tight as during the traditional lift.

4. Upon completing the salto, the legs stretch for the floor. The right leg contacts the floor and elicits more force for the handspring. The left leg steps forward to aid in positioning the body. In addition, the right leg swings up and over the hands too. Both legs should come together as the body is inverted.

5. The arms must be straight. There is usually an intense stretch of the shoulder region to impart a vertical force to the body. The hands should actually leave the floor during the inverted (perpendicular) position.

6. The head is hyperextended. Visual contact with the floor is a prerequisite for optimal flight and landing.

7. The handspring is the connecting element between both types of saltos. Upon contacting the mat, the legs are usually bent and then very vigorously extended to acquire the necessary vertical height for the subsequent front salto.

8. The arms are thrown up and forward as the hips move more vertically. The tuck is very tight to increase angular velocity.

9. Both feet contact the floor together. The hips and knees are flexed to absorb the impact of the landing.

10. The arms are carried forward and placed on the mat. As the arms bend, the hips are flexed. As the hips move over the hands, both the arms and the hip region are straightened. Once again, the legs are bent upon contacting the mat. The arms should remain above the shoulders throughout the lift of the legs, while airborne, and upon finalizing the sequence.

Front Handspring, Piked Front Salto, Front Handspring

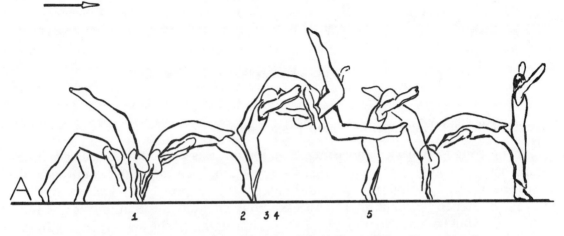

Figure 1-3a: Front Handspring, Piked Front Salto, Front Handspring.

The execution of the piked front salto is highly dependent upon the gymnast's ability to perform excellent front handsprings. This series of tumbling skills requires continuous action of both the arms and the feet. (See Figure 1-3a.) All such moves should be viewed as basically one move (skill) and certainly not three separate skills. Continuity of motion is the key to good tumbling. The main coaching hints are:

1. The hands must leave the mat as the body is in a vertical position. To do otherwise would distract from the flight time and stability upon landing.

2. As the feet contact the mat, the arms are thrown up and forward.

3. The hips assume a flexed position. In this case, the gymnast does not place his hands behind his legs to assume a greater pike. However, it is still a piked front salto.

4. The vertical lift necessary for this skill is greatly dependent upon the vertical lift of the hips.

5. Recovery is realized as the hips are extended to position the feet under the center of gravity. Naturally, the displacement of the center of gravity beyond the points of support is aided by the continued forward movement of the arms in anticipation of the next front handspring.

Figure 1-3b: Round-Off, Back Handspring, Piked Back Salto.

Round-Off Back Handspring, Piked Back Salto

The round-off back handspring combination was previously discussed. The same basic principles are true in this sequence too. The round-off connects and converts forward motion into backward motion. (See Figure 1-3b.) The piked back salto is harder to perform than the back salto in the tuck position, but it is easier than the layout back salto (principle of radius of rotation). The main coaching hints are:

1. The most important factor influencing the performance is the takeoff posi-

tion. The arms must be stretched vertically to assist the body in the necessary upward motion.

2. The pike is quickly acquired as the body approaches its maximal vertical lift. The pike should be deep with the hands behind the knees. However, some gymnasts have used the body position in the illustration. At any rate, it is important to vigorously lift the legs upward toward the chest region. The tighter the pike, the greater the chance for success.

Front Handspring, Cartwheel Aerial

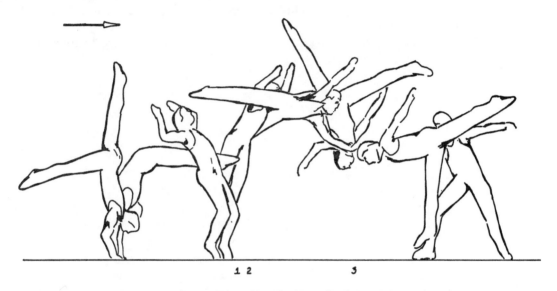

Figure 1-4:   Front Handspring, Cartwheel Aerial.

Once again, the front handspring is used as the skill to impart the necessary force to a subsequent skill (cartwheel aerial). This skill is actually a cartwheel without hands. (See Figure 1-4.) It is a good combination for free exercise sequences. The main coaching hints are:

1. Upon finishing the front handspring, the arms should be carried high above the shoulders.

2. The takeoff position should be just past vertical. Both feet are used to attain the necessary vertical momentum. The left foot trails the right leg since the latter is quickly moved back-upward. The left leg serves to assist in acquiring the desirable vertical-horizontal position noted in the illustration.

3. The right leg leads the direction of motion while the head is hyperextended to aid visual contact with the mat. As the right leg stretches for the mat, the head and chest are lifted back-upward. The left leg assumes contact with the mat to help stabilize the landing.

REFERENCES

Boone, Tommy. "Biomechanics of a Full-Twisting Back Salto," *Scholastic Coach,* (November, 1974a), pp. 84-86.

Boone, Tommy. "Practical Biomechanics for Gymnastic Coaches and Teachers," *Journal of Physical Education,* (March-April, 1974b), pp. 195-207.

Boone, Tommy. "High School Gymnastics," *The North Carolina Journal,* Vol. 10, No. 2, (April, 1974c), pp. 22-23.

Hay, James G. *The Biomechanics of Sports Techniques.* Englewood Cliffs, N.J.: Prentice-Hall, Inc., 1973.

Jensen, Clayne R., and Gordon W. Schultz. *Applied Kinesiology.* New York: McGraw Hill Book Company, 1970.

Rasch, Phillip J., and Roger K. Burke. *Kinesiology and Applied Anatomy.* Philadelphia: Lea and Febiger, 1967.

2

Floor Exercise

Floor exercise has become an extremely popular event in gymnastics. The interest is primarily a result of a better free exercise area. That is, more schools either have a free exercise mat or have access to such a mat. In the past, this event was practiced on hardwood floors which frequently resulted in bruises of the feet, shin splits, and a poor attitude toward floor exercise. Fortunately, the present use of a mat corrects these problems. In addition, the gymnast can more fully concentrate on conveying his unique qualities (flexibility, strength, explosive tumbling, exciting combinations, and/or impressive execution) which are eye-catching.

TRAINING FOR FLOOR EXERCISE

Floor exercise is the next logical step in executing tumbling skills in combination with almost unlimited variations in body movement. The movements (skills) are limited only by the gymnast's lack of imagination and/or physical ability.

Training for floor exercise competition starts with an open mind and hard physical work. The use of films is encouraged by many coaches. They often increase one's awareness of different tumbling combinations and transitions between the tumbling sequences. To begin with, all gymnasts must have some exposure to a tumbling program. Then, the coach can vary floor exercise workouts depending upon his objectives. For example, if his objective is to develop tumbling sequences, it may be necessary to practice a particular sequence or combination more frequently than a similar amount of work on transitional skills. When necessary, depending on the prerequisites of a specific skill, a gymnast may supplement his normal workout with flexibility or strength development exercises. In fact, it is the author's contention that the greatest single factor enhancing floor exercise work-outs is flexibility. Hence, work at being flexible and the skills will be accomplished much easier. Some general, but important training hints are:

1. Be aware of individual differences. Don't make every gymnast adhere to one specific routine. Encourage individuality. Utilize unique qualities such as flexibility or one's ability to be explosive and dynamic. Arrange routines so that weaknesses are not noticeable; whereas, strengths would be evident.

2. Work on transitional (corner) moves. Traditionally, gymnasts have failed to smoothly combine one sequence with another sequence. If necessary, invent a new move, but at least do something encouraging.

3. The first and last sequences of the floor exercise routine must be dynamic and eye-catching. This is obviously the reason for the introduction of the double back salto at the beginning of a routine and the common double twisting back salto as an ending.

4. Too often gymnasts have failed to fully utilize the floor exercise area. The floor design should be cautiously examined to insure desirable variations and continuity of movement.

5. Gymnasts often miss static positions and moves of strength. In both cases, the major problem is lack of flexibility or training. Therefore, train for increased flexibility to lessen the strain on the hamstrings when performing, e.g., a side scale. Also, when using a straight-straight press, the wider the legs can be spread the easier the press.

6. With heart disease as prevalent as it is among predominately the middle-aged individuals, there is a need to utilize the aerobic system to help diminish the impact of the coronary risk factors such as overweightness, high blood pressure, high blood fats, etc. It is possible that floor exercise can be effectively used to increase the performer's cardio-respiratory endurance. This is important in that generally most coaches acknowledge an activity of this nature as being basically a byproduct of one's muscular strength and endurance. It is also important to realize that with an enhanced heart and circulatory system, there would seem to be a greater store of available energy for muscular performance (Briney, 1970).

Although there are a variety of activities that stimulate the cardio-respiratory system for a period of time sufficiently long to produce a training effect, the conventional approach to conditioning in gymnastics fails to produce a training effect as it concerns the heart. But since performing a sequence or routine is dependent upon, to an extent, the heart, lungs, and circulatory system, as well as the muscular system, a suggested conditioning approach to floor exercise is presented for the reader's consideration.

Break the FX (floor exercise) routine into four or five parts. Perform the first part two to three times, rest for thirty seconds to a minute, and then repeat. Do each part accordingly; however, vary the rest interval depending upon the nature of the skills in each part. Later, divide the routine into two halves, repeat each half two times, rest for a minute to a minute and thirty seconds, and repeat. Use the same approach for the second half. As the muscular and cardio-respiratory systems accommodate the stress, perform the routine as a whole, rest three minutes and repeat (Maddux, 1970).

Many performers in essentially anaerobic activities such as weight-lifting, tennis, sprinting, and gymnastics are also supplementing their respective workouts with long distance running to increase their capacity to use oxygen.

7. Don't stress performing the difficult skills until the gymnasts are ready. Good execution of an intermediate routine is better than poor execution of a difficult routine. Learn the basic and intermediate tumbling and transitional skills before attempting the advanced skills.

FLOOR EXERCISE SKILLS

The floor exercise skills are presented in three illustrations which collectively encompass a floor exercise routine. The routine is composed of five sequences. Each sequence consists of tumbling and transitional skills.

The first and second sequences are combined in Figure 2-1. The first sequence consists of a tumbling series (a pike front salto step out, round-off back handspring, pike Arabian salto) and several transitional moves (Swedish fall, immediate one-half turn to a straddle stand, straight-straight press to handstand). The second sequence consists of tumbling skills (round-off cartwheel aerial, cartwheel) and corner moves (pivot, scale). The main coaching hints are:

1. Keep the tumbling skills moving—don't hesitate. Continuity of motion is an important step toward achieving success.

2. The first sequence is dynamic. The coach should stress (in this and similar sequences) a smooth transition from the front salto into the round-off. The latter must assist the back handspring in gaining sufficient vertical momentum necessary for an effective execution of the Arabian salto.

3. The Swedish fall is very quick. The upward lift of the hips rotate around the support arm (left). The movement stops in a straddle stand position from which a straight-straight press is used to attain the handstand position. At this point, the gymnast should hold the handstand. It must be straight (shoulders extended, head between the arms, straight back and legs) like an arrow and not curved like a bow.

4. In the second sequence, the aerial is performed with a slightly open hip position. That is, the left hip will generally drop backward to facilitate the back-upward lift of the body. An excellent technique for spotting this skill is to place one hand at the hip region and one hand between the left shoulder and lower back. The objective of the spotter would be to give the tumbler the necessary vertical lift as well as preventing him from casting too far backwards.

5. The right foot must stretch for the mat and support the body weight until the left foot contacts the mat and transfers the momentum to the outstretched arms.

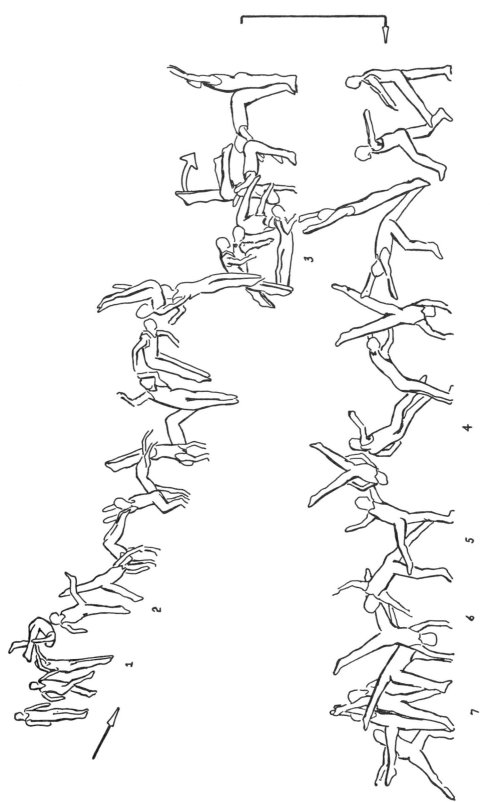

Figure 2-1: The First and Second Sequences of an Illustrated Floor Exercise Routine.

6. During the cartwheel, the arms and legs must remain straight. The head should be positioned so that one can see the floor. The right leg is piked to allow contact with the mat. Placement of the foot should be close to the right hand.

7. As the body is straightened vertically, the arms move to an overhead position. The left leg assumes the weight as the right leg swings forward and backward with the turning of the body on the left leg (bent-knee position). Not shown in the illustration is a side scale (the last skill of this sequence).

The third and fourth sequences are combined in Figure 2-2. The third sequence consists of what is generally termed front tumbling (run, front handspring, pike front salto, front handspring) and transitional moves (Swedish fall, neck spring with one-half twist to front support). The fourth sequence consists of tumbling and floor exercise skills (run, diving forward roll, headspring to knees, press-kick to handstand, pirouette, snap down from handstand). The main coaching hints are:

1. The takeoff position (arms and shoulders) for the front handspring must be vertical.

2. Entry into the pike front salto is achieved by a vigorous upward motion of the arms. As the head is flexed, the hips assume the responsibility of attaining the necessary vertical lift. By delaying the quick flexion of the body during the takeoff, the gymnast will attain greater height. Grasping the legs decreases the radius of rotation resulting in an increased angular velocity (a faster spin).

3. Once again, the arms remain outstretched in anticipation of the next front handspring. As the body arches over, the head should be held backward and not flexed forward. This technique enhances the landing and subsequent skills.

4. The hips are raised to position the body for the neckspring. As the hips approach the base of support, the legs are extended up and forward. The arms are also extended—a movement which helps to elicit the one-half twist. Then, the body is controlled as it is lowered to the mat in a front support position. The hips are raised, drawing the feet in close to the hands. As the feet absorb the body weight, the body is straightened with the arms in an overhead position.

5. The fourth sequence begins with a small run, hurdle, and diving forward roll. The arms should be used to lift the body during the takeoff and to absorb the initial impact upon landing. It is important that the head is flexed very quickly upon landing.

6. The front handspring begins as the outstretched hands contact the mat. The arms bend while the forehead contacts the mat. As the hips move beyond the hands, a quick extension of the body and arms is evident. However, instead of landing on the feet, the legs are flexed at the knees. The feet and then the knees contact the mat (almost at the same time). This is a very easy skill to learn. A spotter should place his right hand under the back of the participant to control his descent and stability.

7. The arms move forward and support the body for a semi-press to a handstand. However, the right arm is moved a one-half turn (pirouette) to a momentary

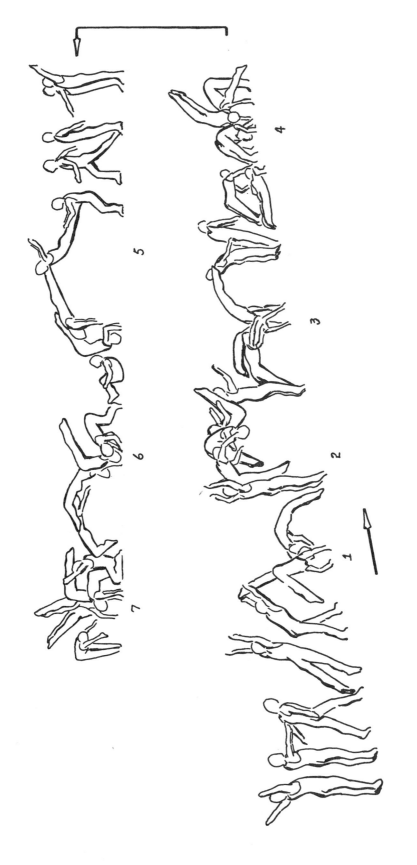

Figure 2-2: The Third and Fourth Sequences of an Illustrated Floor Exercise Routine.

handstand from which a snap down is executed. Then assume an erect position for continuation of the exercise.

The fifth and final sequence is illustrated in Figure 2-3. The closing sequence consists of a final tumbling combination (run, round-off back handspring, full-twisting back salto). The main coaching hints are:

1. The hurdle must be diagonal and not vertical. The greater height a gymnast achieves in this case, the less force upon entry into the round-off. (Refer to Chapter 1 for more coaching hints relative to the round-off back handspring.) Simply stated, both must be smoothly executed and goal directed.

2. The full-twisting back salto begins with the vertical lift at takeoff. The most important objective is to complete the twist at the inverted position as noted in Figure 2-3. The twisting action is enhanced as the arms are moved in closer to the body. Conversely, extending the arms upon finishing the twist aids in stopping the twisting action. If necessary, at the beginning, envision the full twist in two parts: (1) a back dive with a one-half twist; and (2) a barani out to the feet. The mat should be visible throughout the full-twisting back salto.

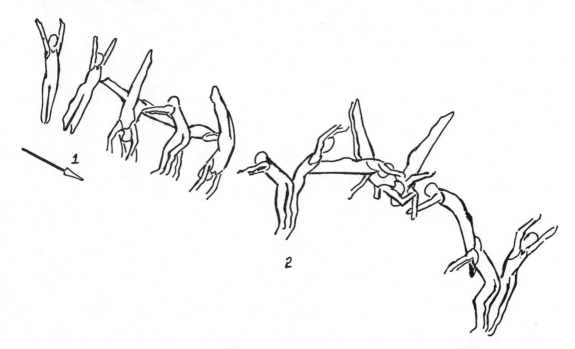

Figure 2-3:   The Fifth and Final Sequence of an Illustrated Floor Exercise Routine.

Although floor exercise is easily adaptable to the skill level of the participant, all participants must adhere to the same basic biomechanics underlying springing and tumbling skills for aesthetically pleasing execution.

It behooves the coach to instruct his gymnasts as to the correct method of (1) attaining lift and rotation at the instant of takeoff, (2) controlling rotation while airborne, and (3) dissipating the force of impact.

With regard to static positions, the gymnast must endeavor to either (1) keep his center of weight directly over the center of the base of support, (2) lower the center of gravity, or (3) enlarge the area of the base.

In summary, it is also important that the floor exercise routine corresponds to the ability level of the participants. Correct biomechanics, imagination, and hard work are prerequisites for an artistic performance.

REFERENCES

Briney, Kenneth L. *Cardiovascular Disease: A Matter of Prevention.* Belmont, California: Wadsworth Publishing Company, Inc., 1970.

Cooper, Kenneth H. *The New Aerobics.* New York, N.Y.: Bantam Books, Inc., 1972.

Hughes, Eric. *Gymnastics for Men.* New York: The Ronald Press Company, 1966.

Maddux, Gordon T. *Men's Gymnastics.* Pacific Palisades, California: Goodyear Publishing Company, Inc., 1970.

3

Side Horse

The side horse is generally accepted as the most difficult event in gymnastics. This applies to not only side horse training, but also the execution of side horse skills in competition. Hence, a coach should make sure that his gymnasts train properly to attain the adaptation necessary for optimum performance.

TRAINING FOR SIDE HORSE

Side horse training has received very little attention in the past. Generally, a gymnast unable to compete on the parallel bars or the rings (perhaps due to a lack of strength) would devote considerable attention to specifically the side horse, which requires balance. Consequently, the highly specialized training and concentration often resulted in a single gymnast with advanced skills on the side horse. This method, however, is not a desirable approach to gymnastic training. All gymnasts must designate a portion of their time to each event in gymnastics.

Training for the side horse requires that the performer concentrates on and develops the prerequisites for safe and desirable execution of side horse skills. For such side horse skills as travels, loops, doubles, and scissors, it is necessary that a gymnast: (1) concentrates on keeping his arms and legs straight; (2) develops strong and supple shoulder, forearm and arm, abdominal, hip, and gluteal muscles; and (3) correctly applies the principles of dynamic balance as illustrated when the shoulders lean laterally, forward or backward, and combinations of these to better position the center of gravity over or near the base of support (either one or both hands).

It may be useful to analyze specific skills by breaking them down into their

59022
WILLIAM WOODS COLLEGE LIBRARY

basic parts. Design exercises to induce the correct kinesthetic feeling at the shoulders, hips, and legs as they move through the desired range of motion. Once the gymnast realizes what it is he must do, then appropriate limb and total body movements will be forthcoming with practice. It is much better to work with fundamentals than to hastily move to more advanced, yet poorly executed skills.

Training should be directed toward developing continuous movement. There should be no stops, pauses, or jerks. In addition, the type of skills to be performed have a definite influence on the execution appearance. For example, some skills are performed more slowly (single leg skills) than others (double leg circles).

Negating the speed of execution, however, one must perform each skill to its fullest and in such a way that it enhances the next skill. Double leg circles should blend into turns and travels. Scissors should have a rhythmic appearance into and out of other circular movements.

Finally, gymnasts must realize that body types (short arms and legs vs. long arms and legs) can either help or hinder the acquisition of side horse skills. The latter apparently has the advantage over the former body type. They should also recognize that side horse training frequently results in bruises (ankles and knees) and forearm splints. One must anticipate these outcomes and attempt to handle them as quickly as possible. Wrist bands may help alleviate some of the strain at the wrist joints. The use of warm-up pants can reduce the ankle and knee injuries. As well, when necessary, spotters should certainly be used to assist and aid the performer.

SIDE HORSE SKILLS

Front Support

The performer's hands are placed on the pommels. The arms are fully locked. The legs rest against the horse. They are straight and together.

Rear Support

Naturally the back of the legs will rest against the horse since the rear support is essentially the reverse of the front support.

Feint Support

This support position is usually used to swing into a double leg circle. For example, the performer's right leg is positioned forward while the left leg remains in back of the horse. In this case, the right arm is straight and supports the body slightly above the right pommel. The left arm aids in balance by supporting the upper lean of the shoulders toward the left pommel. Initiation of the swing by the right leg backward to continue with the left leg results in the beginnings of a double leg circle.

Alternate Leg Cuts

Using the front support position discussed previously, cut the left leg under the left hand, and then the right leg under the right hand. What kind of support are you in now? That's right—a rear support position. To move back to a front support position, you must cut the left leg back under the left hand, and the right leg under the right hand. It is very important to keep the support arm straight when supporting the body as a leg moves forward or backward. Alternate leg cuts may be performed between the pommels (saddle), on the left side of the performer (neck), or on the opposite end of the horse (croup).

Single Leg Circle

Using the front support position, circle the left leg under the left hand and then under the right hand back to the FS (front support) position. In contrast to the alternate leg cuts, which are "tick-tock action," the single leg circle implies a continuous movement or circle. It, too, may be performed on the neck, saddle, or croup.

It isn't necessary to always begin with the left leg to the left. A gymnast might decide to start with the right leg to the right side. Also, as the hips begin to move toward the left, the right leg can move between the left leg and the horse to complete a circle.

Single Leg Stockli Mount

Standing and facing the horse, the performer places the left hand on the neck (end of the horse) and the right hand on the near pommel with a reverse grip. It is necessary to jump toward the saddle with the right leg moving up and over the croup and between the pommels. The right arm supports the jump and one-half turn on the near pommel as the left arm pushes against the end of the horse to aid in positioning the hips between the pommels. The left hand moves to the far pommel to support the body as the right leg now continues to circle over the horse. The released right hand now regrasps the pommel to finish in a straight-arm, rear support position.

Balance is the key to good side horse work. It is the ability of the performer to control himself while in motion. Whereas the parallel bar performer controls a handstand (static balance), the side horse performer must never stop and yet maintain balance (dynamic balance).

Maddux (1970) suggests that the performer should decrease the length of time that one hand acts as the base to diminish the problems encountered with maintaining dynamic balance. Fast hands and dynamic balance appear to make working the side horse a little easier.

The side horse skills are not thought to be as easily identified as skills performed on the parallel bars or some other apparatus. The difficulty comes from the blending of one skill into another skill. Thus, it appears to the beginner that there is no exact beginning and/or ending to most side horse skills. Naturally these skills can be performed separately or in combination with other skills. The illustrated side horse routine is analyzed to specifically clarify the ambiguity apparent with some side horse terminology.

It behooves the beginner side horse coach to thoroughly examine a book entitled *The Side Horse* by Don Tonry (printed by Nissen Corp., 1966). The terminology and the classification of side horse movements are greatly simplified. The photographs of specific movements with the correct terminology can't help but assist a concerned coach. In additon, a detailed mechanical analysis of several popular side horse skills appears in Part IV.

Loop (1-5), Double Leg Circles (6-14), Moore Without Pommels (15-18)

The main coaching hints (see Figure 3-1) are:

1. The initial motion of the shoulders is in the direction of the horse.

2. As a result, the arms must straighten to support the body. The hips move closer to the base of support. At this point, the hips rotate outward drawing the right hip in close to the right hand.

3. The right arm and shoulder musculature supports the upper body as the hips are extended. The shoulder continues to lean to the right to avoid displacing the center of gravity too far from the base.

4. Both arms support the body as the legs pass over the pommels. The upper body leans backward. The head is slightly flexed to aid in maintaining dynamic balance.

5. The left arm supports the body. It leans to the left as the legs move back to the original position.

6. In anticipation of the subsequent skill, the shoulders lean forward first and then laterally second. Both adjustments insure a continuation of dynamic equilibrium.

7. As the right arm and shoulder lean to the right, the left arm and shoulder are raised to aid and allow continuous motion of the legs. The hips are slightly flexed to reduce the resistance to motion.

8. As the legs and hips are stretched out over the horse, the lean is to the right.

9-10. As the legs move in front of the body, both arms support the movement. The head is still slightly flexed to negate the possibility of backward motion.

11. Note the lateral lean of the left shoulder as the legs pass over the end of the horse.

12. Both shoulders must lean forward to counteract the backward pull of the legs (weight). Hence, as the center of gravity is kept as possible to the base, dynamic balance is maintained.

13-14. Refer to numbers 6-12 (the mechanics are the same).

15. The hips are flexed to increase the velocity of the movement. The left arm must lean to the left to help elevate the hips.

16. As the legs swing over the pommels, the placement of the right arm and

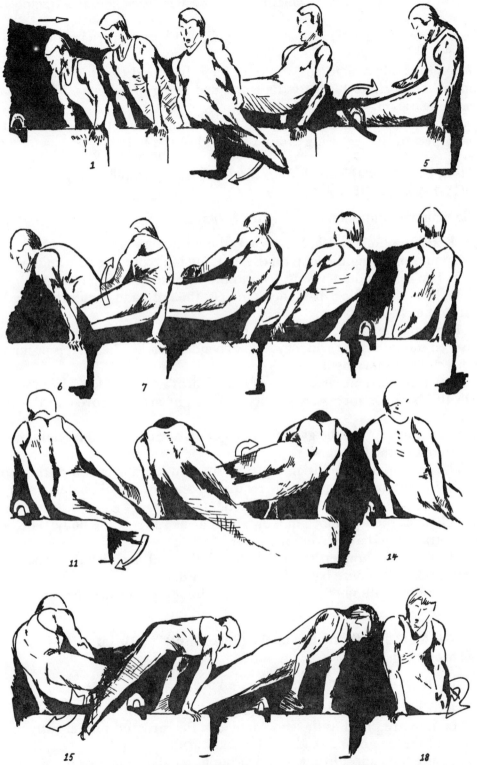

Figure 3-1: Loop (1-5), Double Leg Circles (6-14), Moore Without out Pommels (15-18).

the already supporting left arm maintains stability by leaning forward over the end of the horse.

17. As the body straightens, the right hand is moved to a more appropriate position on the horse to facilitate the continued swing of the legs. The left arm must remain straight.

18. Once the right arm contacts the horse, it must support the body during the final aspect of the leg swing around the end of the horse.

Loop (1-4), Uphill (side) Travel (5-8), Circle (9-10), Downhill (side) Travel (11-14), Loop (15-16)

The main coaching hints (see Figure 3-2) are:

1-4. Refer to numbers 1,5, Figure 3-1 (the mechanics are the same).

5. Upon completing the loop on the end, the hips continue to swing over the pommels. The right shoulder must lean to the right to reduce tension in the left side of the body. As the legs pass the pommels, the left hand is quickly placed on the near pommel.

6. The shoulders must now lean to the left as the legs swing over the end of the horse. At this point, the arm may tend to bend. Fight it. The head is positioned in the direction of movement.

7. Notice the extreme lateral lean of the left arm and shoulder. The hips move closer to the base for increased balance. The right arm is moved to the same pommel.

8. Both arms support the gymnast's weight on one pommel. The right hand is placed in front of the left hand.

9. The left hip also begins an outward rotation in anticipation of the movement over the second pommel. This requires a shift of the shoulders from the inside of the pommel to the outside position.

10. Then, as the legs move in front, both arms support the body. The body should be straight and away from the horse.

11-14. Refer to numbers 5-8. The downhill travel is easier than the uphill travel, but both skills utilize basically the same mechanics.

15-16. Refer to numbers 1-5, Figure 3-1 (the mechanics are the same).

Circle (1-2), Moore Without Pommels (3-6), Circle (7-8), Loop (9-12), Back Kehre-in (13-16)

The main coaching hints (see Figure 3-3) are:

1-2. Refer to numbers 6-14, Figure 3-1 (the mechanics are the same).

3. The hips are piked as the shoulders lean forward and turn slightly to the right. Most of the weight is already on the right arm.

4-5. Notice the almost hyperextended position (elbow joint) of the right arm as the body is straightened over the pommels. The left arm must move very quickly

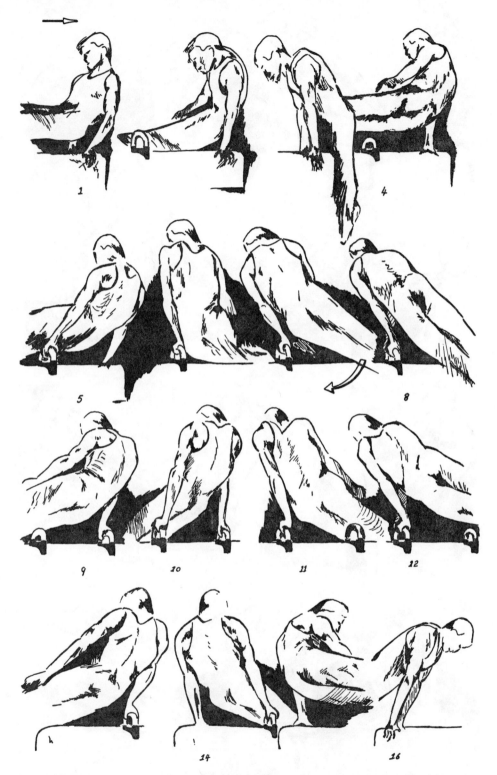

Figure 3-2: Loop (1-4), Uphill (side) Travel (5-8), Circle (9-10), Downhill (side) Travel (11-14), Loop (15-16).

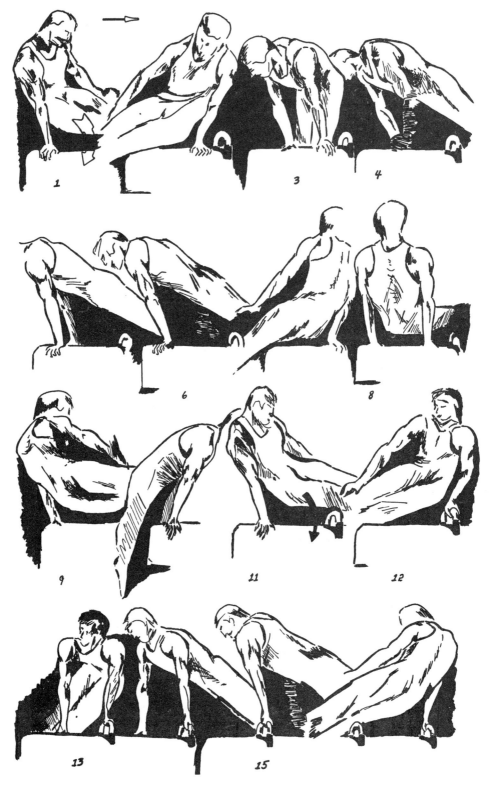

Figure 3-3: Circle (1-2), Moore Without Pommels (3-6), Circle (7-8), Loop (9-12), Back Kehre-in (13-16).

to the end of the horse. Then, the weight is transferred from the right arm to the left arm.

6. Only the left arm supports the body. The right arm advances to a position near the pommel. This is more easily accomplished as the legs descend around the end of the horse.

7-8. Refer to numbers 6-14, Figure 3-1 (the mechanics are the same).

9-11. Refer to numbers 1-5, Figure 3-1 (the mechanics are the same).

12. The loop on the end must result in a continued forward motion of the shoulders (particularly the left shoulder and arm) as the legs circle the horse. The left arm will come to support the gymnast's position.

13. The hips must assume a deep pike to increase the velocity of the movement. The right arm aids in keeping the upper body supported. However, at this point, the left arm is under greater stress than the right arm.

14. As the hips straighten, the arms simply support the body. The left side leads into the skill. Less weight is on the right arm.

15. The left arm and shoulder musculature supports the body as it completes the swing over the pommels. Due to the new position of the gymnast, the right arm is quickly moved to the right pommel.

16. As the right hand grasps the pommel, it begins to assume the weight of the body and control of the skill. The shoulders lean to the right to maintain dynamic balance.

Circles (1-5), Moore, Immediate Moore (6-11), Circle, Break into Reverse Scissors (12-17)

The main coaching hints (see Figure 3-4) are:

1-5. Refer to numbers 6-14, Figure 3-1 (the mechanics are the same).

6. As the legs pass over the pommel, the gymnast must take on a vigorous pike (which reduces the radius of rotation, increasing the velocity of the movement). The elbows may appear to be slightly hyperextended (at this point) since the arms *must* support the upper body as it leans forward.

7. Very quickly the body is straightened (action-reaction). The shoulder lean is still evident due to the necessity of keeping the center of gravity near or over the pommel (base of support).

8. As the legs swing around to pass over the pommel, the left arm is released. The body pivots around the right arm.

9-11. Refer to numbers 6-8 (the mechanics are the same).

12-13. Refer to numbers 6-14, Figure 3-1 (the mechanics are the same).

14. Upon almost completing the circle, the left leg remains in front of the horse as the right leg moves to a position behind the horse.

15. The downward swing to the left positions the body, allowing the right leg to pass forward over the horse as the left leg is passed backward to a high position above the horse.

16-17. As the body swings to the right, the back leg is advanced forward as the front leg is raised and moves to a position in back of the horse.

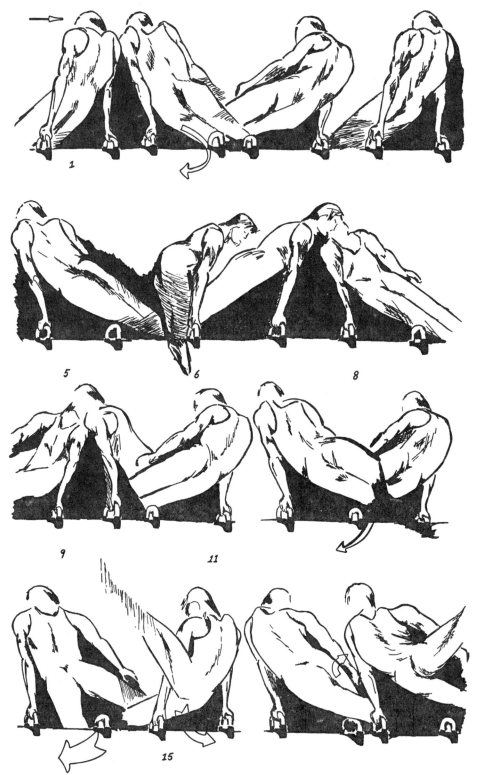

Figure 3-4: Circles (1-5), Moore, Immediate Moore (6-11), Circle Break into Reverse Scissors (12-17).

Front Scissors (1-9), Circle (10-12), Downhill (side) Travel (13-15), Loop (16-17)

The main coaching hints (see Figure 3-5) are:

1. The raised (right) leg moves to a back position as the left leg (which was in back of the horse) moves to a front position.

2. The left leg descends and then lifts, raising the hips.

3. The left arm is raised in anticipation of the backward motion of the left leg. The support (right) arm leans to the right to counteract the upward lift to the left.

4. Both legs descend and swing to the right. At the peak of the swing, the right leg moves forward. The hips swing back to the left as the right hand contacts the pommel.

5-6. The upward motion of the body results in a loss of grip (left hand). The front (right) leg moves to the back of the horse. The back (left) leg moves in front of the horse.

7-8. After the swing to the right, the left leg moves backward and the back leg moves forward.

9. The left leg moves in front of the horse to join the right leg in swinging to the right into a double leg circle.

10-12. Refer to numbers 6-14, Figure 3-1 (the mechanics are the same).

13. As the legs swing over the pommel (in front of the left hand), naturally, the left shoulder must lean to the left to draw the center of gravity in closer to the base (which is certainly a very narrow base at that).

14-15. As the legs swing over the end of the horse, the left hand is placed on the horse to assume responsibility for supporting the body as the legs pass over the rear pommel. Hence, the right hand must release the pommel to permit continuation of the swing.

16-17. Refer to numbers 1-5, Figure 3-1 (the mechanics are the same).

Loop, Immediate Circle Without Pommels (1-5), Moore Without Pommels (6-8), Loop to Front Vault Dismount (9-12)

The main coaching hints (see Figure 3-6) are:

1-5. Refer to numbers 1-14, Figure 3-1 (the mechanics are the same).

6-7. The right arm supports the body and maintains dynamic balance by keeping straight and leaning to the right. The left arm advances to the end of the horse as the body is straightened over the pommels. Note the forward lean of the arms.

8. As the hips swing down and around the end of the horse, the left hand is raised and the right hand is moved to a position near the pommel.

9. As the swing passes the horse, the left hand supports the body again. Obviously, the right hand is raised as the legs pass over the pommel. The hips are flexed and the head (neck) is slightly flexed.

10. As the legs complete the loop, the hips are flexed and are moving upward with the aid of the downward push of both arms.

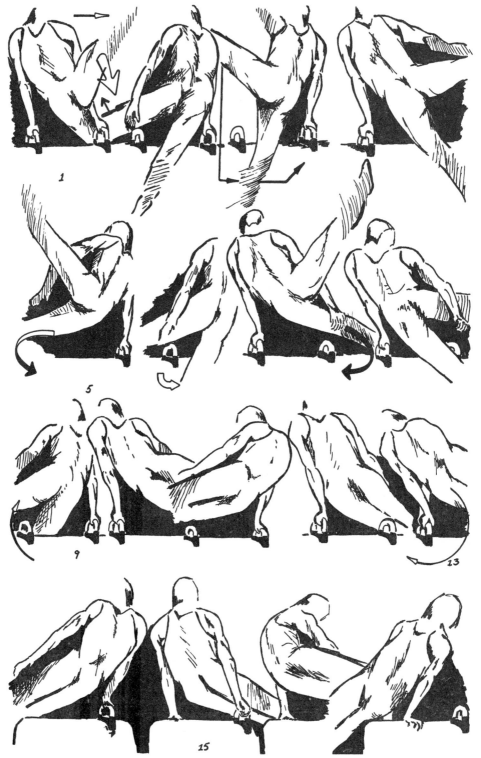

Figure 3-5: Front Scissors (1-9), Circle (10-12), Downhill Travel (13-15), Loop (16-17).

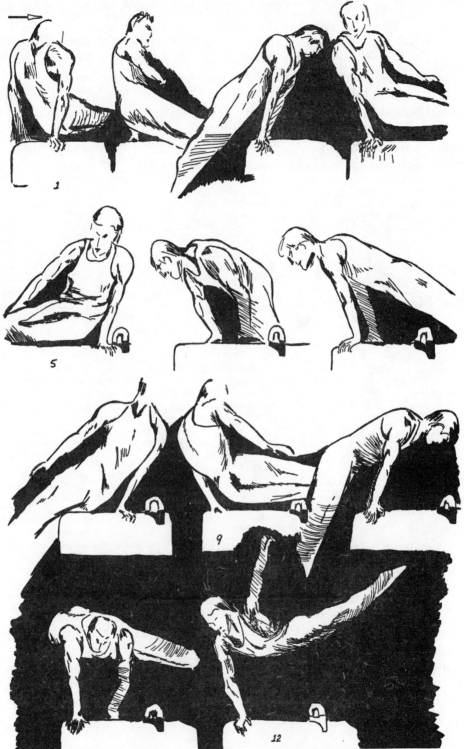

Figure 3-6: Loop, Immediate Circle Without Pommels (1-5), Moore Without Pommels (6-8), Loop to Front Vault Dismount (9-12).

11. The legs attain a position on the same plane as the hips. The right arm supports the body and continues to lift the body as well. The left arm assumes less responsibility and finally is raised above and away from the horse.

12. The deep pike is quickly converted to a slightly hyperextended position at the back (lumbar spine). The body is slightly arched. It is still supported by the right hand. The left arm is above the shoulders. It aids in the lift via the transfer of momentum from part to whole. The upper body remains somewhat motionless as the lower limbs and hips begin to descend for landing.

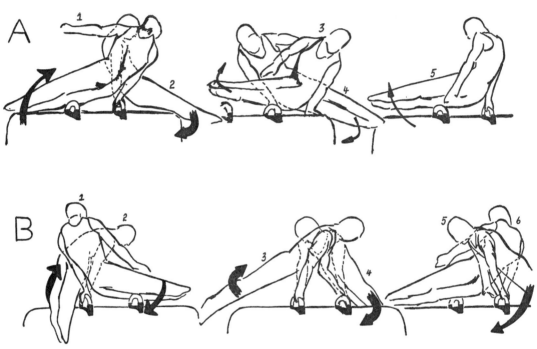

Figure 3-7:   Stockli (A), Russian Moore (B). Analyze these two skills.

To determine your ability to analyze specific skills, examine Figure 3-7 and note the main coaching hints for both skills (A—Stockli, and B—Russian Moore). List your main points of concern on a sheet of paper and then refer to the text of the chapter for similar moves. You may discover whether your analysis is relatively general (gross body movement) or somewhat more detailed (realizing what to look for and quickly determining if such movements are correct). Good luck.

REFERENCES

Maddux, Gordon T. *Men's Gymnastics.* Pacific Palisades, California: Goodyear Publishing Company, Inc., 1970.

Tonry, Don. *The Side Horse.* Cedar Rapids, Iowa: Nissen Corp., 1966.

4

Vaulting

The major difference between vaulting and other gymnastic events is the execution of a single skill rather than a combination of skills. Naturally, the duration of execution of a long horse vault is extremely short when compared to other gymnastic events. For example, to perform a vault over the long horse, the duration of the movement will consist of approximately 2 seconds from takeoff to landing. However, to perform the peach basket (felge) on the parallel bars, the duration of the movement will consist of approximately 6 seconds from handstand to handstand. Obviously not all parallel bar movements are of this duration (e.g., "L" support is held for 1 second), but certainly the execution of 11 skills formulating a routine consists of 30 to 40 seconds.

TRAINING FOR VAULTING

Vaulting is also distinguished from other gymnastic events by its division into seven sequentially related events or phases: (1) run; (2) hurdle; (3) takeoff; (4) preflight; (5) push-off; (6) afterflight; and (7) landing. The key to excellent vaulting lies in the efficient integration of all these phases. Hence, vaulting may be viewed as a routine consisting of seven skills. Just as one must practice each skill in an apparatus routine, the same is true for vaulting. The gymnast should practice each phase as he would normally practice each skill comprising a routine. The information presented relative to each phase is for the purpose of clarification as to their involvement in the performance of vaulting.

Run

A gymnast needs as much linear momentum as possible to effectively perform vaults requiring optimum vertical and horizontal momentum. The motion of the legs and arms produce the necessary linear motion of the total body. A poor manipulation of the arms and legs often distracts from optimum horizontal velocity; consequently, the vaulter is unable to fulfill the technical requirements of vaulting.

In this regard, Bowers, et al, (1972) states that a vaulter should: (1) run on his toes; (2) lean forward as he runs; (3) flex his hips and legs (with the knees high in front); (4) swing the arms back and forward (not diagonally); (5) reach maximum velocity some four steps prior to hurdling; (6) shift the eyes from the board to the horse as he starts to hurdle; and (7) measure and mark off the distance of the run relative to each type of vault. In essence, the run-up should emulate the effective style of sprinters striving to accomplish a specific objective.

A coach cannot overestimate the importance of the run and approach. Without it, vaulting is impossible. With a less than the best run, vaulting is poor. With an overflow of talent for sprinting, however, the performer has a distinct advantage over his opponent with less sprinting skill.

Hurdle

It has been said that the hurdle is a link between the run and the takeoff (Hay, 1973). This is true, but so are all the phases of vaulting except the run and the landing. For example, one may conclude that the push-off is a transitional step between the preflight phase and the afterflight phase. Nevertheless, proper execution of the hurdle is often emotionally stressful due to the maximum velocity attained from the run. This is often the reason why some gymnasts slow their running pace upon approaching the beat board. The gymnast must synchronize movements of the arms, legs, hips, and eyes.

The hurdle consists of lifting one leg, driving from the other leg, and subsequently landing with both feet on the Reuther board. This is followed immediately by a blocking action in which the gymnast converts linear movement into the vigorous vertical movement referred to as the takeoff. The gymnast would do well to remember that he may lose some of his horizontal momentum if the hurdle is too high.

The blocking action (actually a consummation of the hurdle) serves to position the center of gravity in front of the performer's hips, but behind his feet. Hence, the direction of movement for the center of gravity is primarily diagonal as it passes over the feet. The flexed hips and legs are extended (including ankles) and the arms are thrust forward-upward to facilitate the preflight phase (Bowers, et al, 1972).

Takeoff

The takeoff provides the necessary vertical, horizontal, and angular momentum as needed for the preflight of specific vaults. An average time for takeoff from the board is 0.13 seconds.

Hay (1973) states that a slight backward lean as the feet contact the board increases the time on the board. This results in an increased vertical velocity. Since too much backward lean tends to reduce the horizontal velocity generated by the run, the gymnast must determine which (horizontal or vertical velocity) is prerequisite for a specific vault. Conversely, too much forward lean (past the vertical line) toward the horse reduces the duration of the takeoff. As a result, the gymnast's vertical velocity decreases accordingly.

Preflight

An integration of near maximum horizontal velocity, vertical velocity, and angular momentum after the performer has completed the takeoff and is airborne is referred to as the preflight phase. This phase must complement the vault in question. Generally, the preflight is indicative of a high body position without extreme hip flexion (piked) or hyperextension (arched). The upward movement of the legs is facilitated by a gradual head flexion (downward rotation of the chin on the chest). The arms are stretched forward awaiting contact with the horse. The eyes are open and looking for a contact point on the horse. In essence, the preflight phase is a highly critical phase of the entire vault.

Push-Off

The major purposes of the push-off phase are: (1) to adhere to the technical requirement to contact the horse; (2) to alter the preflight resulting in a vertical lift off the horse; and (3) to provide additional momentum to the flight (vault).

As the preformer contacts the horse, the arms are straight (elbows locked, laterally rotated), the body is fully extended, and the head is between the arms. The hands become the center of rotation as the gymnast's center of gravity passes over and beyond the point of contact. The continued rotating forward movement is necessary for specific vaults, e.g., handsprings. Conversely, should the push-off convert the forward angular momentum into a backward rotary movement, the modification in angular motion predisposes one to vaults such as a squat or a straddle.

Afterflight

The afterflight is the unraveling phase of the linked series of movements up to and including the support on the horse. The afterflight represents a realization of the summation of forces derived from the run, the takeoff, and the push-off from the horse.

The gymnast is able to alter the afterflight by modifying the radius of rotation depending upon the type of vault. However, the final descent aspect of the afterflight is similar for all vaults (fully extended).

Landing

This phase completes the final phase of vaulting. The perfomer should land on the balls of the feet. The hips and legs should be slightly flexed to help absorb the force of impact. The head should be held erect in accordance with the technical requirements. The arms should be diagonally up.

The landing must be smooth, controlled, and certainly without major adjustments to maintain static balance. The center of gravity must come to rest within the base of support, the feet, to avoid shifting to maintain balance. Since the feet are placed together upon landing (instead of spreading as might be expected when one dismounts from the high bar), the base is very small, requiring consistent practice of all phases for a controlled and effective landing.

VAULTING SKILLS

Squat (on Side Horse)

The performer should use a small run and a two-foot takeoff. As the hands contact the pommels, the hips are raised with flexion at both hip and knee joints. The squat position is held until the feet pass over the horse. Then, the body is straightened as the feet move toward the mat. Upon contacting the mat, the legs flex slightly to land firmly on both feet. *Spotting:* The coach stands on either side of the horse and grasps the performer's wrist as he begins to support himself. If necessary, the spotter should lift the perfomer through the vault (or lower the horse, or use a spring board for extra lift).

Flank (on Side Horse)

The performer should use a small run and a two-foot takeoff. It is important to remember that too large a run (too much linear momentum) will cause the performer to move over the horse without a good support arm. Hence, the feet seldom contact the mat for a good landing. Most of the action takes place above the horse. For example, as the hands contact the pommels, the right hand remains as a support arm while the left arm is raised to allow the body to move over and in front of the horse. Thus, the hand is released on the flanking side. As the body descends to the mat, the right hand will release allowing the performer to land firmly on both feet. *Spotting:* The coach may stand on either side of the horse to spot, but generally the side that the performer is approaching appears to be best. Why? As the spotter grasps the performer's supporting arm at the wrist, it is often necessary to lift and support the beginner or overweight performer through the vault.

Front (on Side Horse)

The approach is similar to the flank vault, but upon passing above the horse the performer rotates his head, shoulders, and hips a one-quarter turn. Thus, the front part of the body faces the top of the horse. The landing is with both feet, with the support arm between the performer and the horse. *Spotting:* The mechanics for spotting are the same as for the flank vault.

Rear (on Side Horse)

The approach is the same as for the flank or front vaults. This vault is essentially the reverse of the front vault in that the rear of the performer passes over the horse. This action requires a release of the left hand so that the legs can pass through, and a continued support by the right hand (in the case of passing the legs over the neck of the horse). Not like the front vault in which the support hand can remain on the pommel until the feet contact the mat, the rear vault requires the support hand to release the pommel quite early in the descent of the legs. *Spotting:* The spotting technique is the same as for the flank or front vault. However, since the support arm must release earlier than the other two vaults, the spotter must anticipate the regrasps of the (in this case) left hand (which was the first hand to release a pommel).

Straddle (on Side Horse)

The performer must attain a small run and takeoff on both feet. The arms move up and forward to contact the pommels. At this time, the hips should be moving up and forward too. As the hips move over the horse, the legs are spread. A forceful push downward by the hands aids in lifting the shoulders and head as the legs move together again in preparation for landing. *Spotting:* The spotter stands in front of the horse prepared to step in, and grasps the performer's arms should he fail to clear the horse successfully.

Straddle (Long Horse, Far End Vault)

This vault is usually the first of such vaults as the squat, stoop, and hecht to be performed over the long horse. Naturally, this vault requires a longer and faster run than the previously discussed vaults (cross horse). At the instant of takeoff, the performer must reach for the far end of the horse. During the reach phase, the feet and hips should be moving up and forward. At the time the hands contact the horse, the performer must push forcefully downward and backward to become airborne with a slight backward rotation of the legs. The descent of the legs is characterized by the straddle position, which is very quickly changed to a together position in preparation for the landing. The legs are slightly flexed upon landing to reduce the force of impact. *Spotting:* The spotter should stand fairly close to the end of the horse ready to reach forward to grasp the upper arm of the performer should he fail to achieve the desired preflight, or perform the necessary mechanics upon leaving the horse (such as raising the upper body to force the legs downward).

Squat (Long Horse, Far End Vault)

The mechanics for the squat vault are very similar to the straddle. The obvious difference is that the legs pass between the arms (during their descent) in a tuck position. Since the performer's moment of inertia is less (due to the tuck as opposed to the straddle) during the descent, it is not necessary to create the same angular displacement realized with the straddle. As the body passes in front of the horse, the performer extends his body.

Stoop (Long Horse, Far End Vault)

This vault, too, is similar to the straddle. However, the legs are straight, following the hands touching the horse. This means that the performer must push more vigorously to attain additional height to permit the feet to clear the end of the horse. The spotting method is the same as for the straddle, which applies to the squat vaults too.

Although there are a variety of vaulting skills, gymnasts often restrict their execution to primarily two vaults. This is not bad provided adequate exposure to other vaulting skills warrants the use of the two best vaults. Recently, gymnasts have progressed beyond the stoops, hechts, and yamashitas to the vaults requiring an additional salto or initiation of one or more twists. Such a trend, however, should not negate the importance of excellent execution of the aforementioned vaults.

Front Handspring

4   3   2   1

Figure 4-1:   Front Handspring.

The front handspring (Figure 4-1) is usually one of the first advanced vaults attempted by the experienced gymnast. The main coaching hints are:

1. The run must be fast, yet controlled. The takeoff consists of a fast upward motion of the hips and feet as the hands stretch forward to contact the horse. By standing between the beat board and the horse, a coach can help the gymnast acquire the desired preflight. Contact points should be at the waist (left hand) and the thigh (right hand).

2. The objective of the preflight phase is to position the gymnast in a handstand on the neck of the horse. The head should be slightly up as the hands contact the horse. Upon contact, a vigorous upward lift is necessary for optimum height. Vega (1970) states that the push-off should occur at approximately a 45 degree angle from the neck and not a 90 degree angle (as generally accepted). The point is that the longer the hands remain in contact with the horse, the less vertical lift realized.

3. As the body is projected forward-vertical, the neck is less hyperextended to facilitate the angular motion necessary for the skill. Hence, the eyes should move gradually from the horse to, perhaps, a more overhead position. It is important that the performer does not flex the neck forward in anticipation of landing. To do so results in bending at the hips and a loss of the desired body position. This phase of the vault can be effectively spotted by supporting the performer's shoulder and low back.

Hecht

Figure 4-2:   Hecht.

The hecht vault (Figure 4-2) is used by intermediate and advanced gymnasts. Until the Yamashita became popular, the hecht was probably the most popular of the competitive vaults. The main coaching hints are:

1. The takeoff from the beat board must be just past vertical. Generally speaking, the takeoff for the handspring and the piked front handspring is not as forward as the hecht vault. The arms are extended during the preflight phase. Again, like the handspring, the hips and legs must be above the shoulders as the body moves over the horse.

2. Upon leaving the horse, the shoulders should be above the hands. The push (action) and the takeoff (reaction) from the horse are very vigorous. The reaction (the upward-forward movement) should accompany a slight lift of the head and shoulders to position the body more horizontally. Bajin (1971) states that a slight pike upon push-off serves to help elevate the upper trunk. In addition, the powerful lift of the arms also aids in acquiring backward rotation of the body (action-reaction). Spotting is carried out as described in Fig. 4-1 with reference to the front handspring.

Hecht (Full Twist)

Figure 4-3:   Hecht (Full Twist).

The full-twisting hecht (Figure 4-3) is a more advanced expression of the previously discussed hecht vault. The run, takeoff, and contact are basically the same as when performing the hecht vault. The obvious difference is evident during the afterflight in which the gymnast must execute a full twist before landing. The main coaching hints are:

1. The initiation of the twist begins upon leaving the horse. A vigorous down-

ward exertion is prerequisite for the vertical-forward lift and twist reaction. Provided a spotter is on the side opposite the twisting action, he can (if properly positioned with the use of mats, etc.) aid in the lift and twist at the same time.

2. The forceful upward motion of the shoulders (particularly the left shoulder) above the horizontal body position (depicted in Step 2, Fig. 4-3) results in a downward displacement of the hips and legs. Naturally, this movement is necessary for a safe landing.

3. Hence, the twist is executed while the body is more diagonal than horizontal to the floor. The left shoulder is raised as the left arm moves behind the body. The right shoulder has a tendency to drop while the right arm is thrown across the chest of the performer. The head is turned in the direction of the twist to enhance the twisting action via the longitudinal axis of the body.

4. The continued attempt to realize where one is to land increases the chances of success. Also, an excellent twist (particularly the hip region) aids in landing correctly. It is often helpful to use a spotter at Step 4 to aid in supporting the body as the turn is completed.

Yamashita

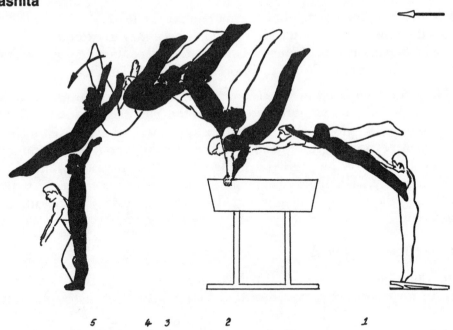

Figure 4-4: Yamashita.

The Yamashita vault (Figure 4-4) is actually a piked front handspring. The run, the takeoff, and the push-off for both vaults are essentially the same. The big difference is in the afterflight. The front handspring arches until landing while the Yamashita vault requires a vigorous pike followed by an arched position before landing. The main coaching hints are:

1. The preflight entails a forceful upward lift of the hips and legs so that the gymnast will contact the horse upon entering the handstand position.

2. The head should be up. The arms must be straight. A slight give and forceful extension of the shoulders often aids in achieving maximum height for optimum execution. The push-off must be fast and goal directed. It must not be too long or too short. Both conditions adversely influence the height of the vault. At this point, a vaulter could push off and land on a trampoline placed in front of the horse.

3. Just after the push-off has occurred, the hips are forcefully flexed. Hence, the name piked front handspring is often used instead of Yamashita. The head position changes to a more natural or slightly flexed position. At this point in the afterflight, it is fairly simple to spot the performer (without the aid of a trampoline) by placing one hand at the shoulder area and the other hand at the mid-back or hip region depending on the height of the vault.

4. In essence, the piked position becomes even tighter since the chest moves upward to the legs. This results in an increased angular velocity due to the shortening of the radius of rotation (tighter pike). The arms are stretched above the shoulders and near the head. They do not contact the legs.

5. As the hips begin to descend, it becomes necessary to extend the hips. This creates an arched appearance, which is continued until contacting the mat, at which time the legs and hips are flexed to absorb the shock of landing.

Bajin (1970) compared gymnasts from different countries in performing the Yamashita vault. He found that the preflight of the Yugoslavian and the Canadian gymnasts (mean, 43.7 degrees) was less than the American gymnasts (mean, 52.3 degrees) when performing the piked front handspring vault. He concluded that the increased height of the preflight of the American gymnasts resulted in a late push-off. Naturally, a late hand release predisposes one to a late pike. This distracts from attaining the optimum height and flight time necessary to execute a good landing.

Yamashita (One-Half Twist)

The Yamashita·with a one-half twist (Figure 4-5) differs from the Yamashita vault by the inclusion of the twist during the afterflight. The main coaching hints are:

1. Due to the necessity in initiating the twist, the left arm is raised more quickly from the horse than the right arm. In this instance, the left arm aids in elevating the left shoulder. Hence, the delayed upward movement of the right arm helps in positioning the right shoulder beneath the left shoulder. In addition, the twist of the head to the right enhances the twisting action.

2. It is important that emphasis is placed first on the vertical lift in the inverted piked position. The head is positioned so that the performer can see his legs as the inverted pike becomes tighter due to the upward motion (flexion of the hips)

4 3 2 1

Figure 4-5:   Yamashita (One-Half Twist).

of the chest, head, and arms. It is only reasonable to expect that a gymnast would learn this move on the trampoline before attempting it over a horse.

3. As the hips gradually rotate downward and/or just after the head is tucked (resulting in a lot of visual contact with the horse), the hips are extended. The body should be straight and the one-half twist completed at horizontal. Ideally, when considering the position of the legs (forming a 180 degree angle), the half twist should be completed at the 90 degree mark. The second 90 degrees (horizontal to the floor) should be used for body correction and preparation for landing.

4. The velocity of the legs and feet is certainly faster than that of the upper body which appears to be rather motionless as the legs descend to a standing position. Actually, a conscious lift (back-upward) of the shoulders, adjunct to a slight hip flexion, is prerequisite for an effective afterflight and landing.

Yamashita (Followed by a Tuck Front Salto)

This vault is another variation of the Yamashita vault. The second salto increases the difficulty of the vault. As a result, certain prerequisites must be met prior to performing this vault. For example, a successful Yamashita vault is an obvious preliminary for attempting a second salto. Also, each phase of the vault must be excellently executed to realize the vertical lift and body position necessary for the second salto. (See Figure 4-6.) The main coaching hints are:

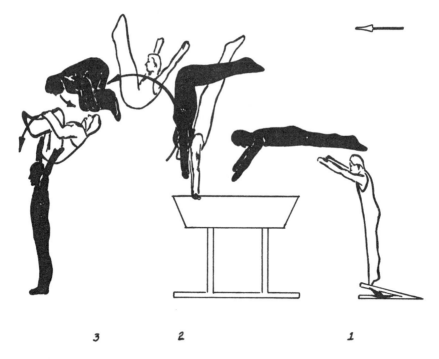

3   *2*   *1*

Figure 4-6:   Yamashita (Followed by Tuck Front Salto).

1. The preflight is similar in execution to the Yamashita vault. However, it is generally much faster and more explosive in appearance. This is due to the increased linear momentum (run), better blocking action (hurdle), and a more vertical lift from the beat board (takeoff). The preflight is finalized upon contacting the horse just short of the handstand position.

2. The push-off phase entails a vigorous upward lift of the body as the hips flex. The upper body is quickly flexed to move closer to the legs. However, as the chest movement is taking place, the hips are forcefully extended (transfer of momentum from part to whole). The initial hip flexion positions the body for an action-reaction motion. That is, due to the hip extension, the movement of the chest toward the legs will be enhanced.

3. As a result, the increased angular momentum coupled with the shortening of the radius of rotation (hip and leg flexion) increases the angular velocity of the second salto. The first salto must be completed at the peak of the afterflight. The second salto is usually completed within the first 90 degrees. The forward wrapping of the arms around the flexed legs aids in securing an additional increase in angular velocity. Naturally, the faster the execution of saltos, the more time gained for proper descent and recognition of landing considerations. Generally, the second 90 degrees is used for body extension and preparation for landing. Indeed, a 100 to 105 degree descent would increase the effectiveness of the standing position.

Tsukahara

4   3   2   1

Figure 4-7:   Tsukahara (Cartwheel with One-Fourth Turn In with
a Back Out).

The Tsukahara vault (Figure 4-7) consists of an initial cartwheel preflight converted into an immediate round-off followed by a back tuck salto and extension upon landing. This vault is relatively new and often performed by gymnasts seeking a different and/or more challenging experience derived from the round-off backout combination. The main coaching hints are:

1. Preflight is finalized as the left hand contacts the horse. Upon contact, the gymnast should be almost in the handstand position. The entire body should be turning to the left beyond the quarter (90 degree—cartwheel) turn to a one-half (180 degree—round-off) turn position.

2. At this point, most of the weight will come to rest on the right arm. Yet, the left arm may quickly slide to the neck of the horse to support the body. The left arm also aids the right arm in generating the necessary vertical force prerequisite for the vault. Hence, strong upper body musculature is imperative.

3. Once airborne, the head is thrown backward as the hips and legs are flexed. Collectively, these adjustments increase angular velocity. The arms move from an overhead position to direct contact with the hamstrings, which causes the tuck to become tighter.

4. The forceful throw of the head backward is probably the second most critical aspect (push-off being the first) of the execution process. Thirdly, the

tucking action complements both the push-off and the head throw. A coach must teach this skill on the trampoline before it is attempted over the horse. The availability of the overhead spotting belts helps to abate undue tension. When it comes time to do it over the horse, the spotter must position himself in such a way (with mats) that he can contact the performer as he goes into the back salto. An alternate method would be catching the performer as he comes out of the salto.

REFERENCES

Bajin, Boris. "Hecht Olympic Compulsory Vault," *The Modern Gymnast,* Vol. 13, No. 2, (November, 1971).

Bajin, Boris. "Yugoslavian and Canadian Gymnasts in Performing the Yamashita Vault," *The Modern Gymnast,* Vol. 12, No. 1, (January, 1970).

Bowers, Carolyn O., Jacquelyn U. Fie, Kitty Kjeldsen, and Andrea B. Schmid. *Judging and Coaching Women's Gymnastics.* Palo Alto, California: National Press Books, 1972.

Hay, James G. *The Biomechanics of Sports Techniques.* Englewood Cliffs, N.J.: Prentice-Hall, Inc., 1973.

Hughes, Eric. *Gymnastics for Men.* New York: The Ronald Press Company, 1966.

Vega, Armando. "Long Horse Vaulting," *The Athletic Journal,* Vol. 51, No. 4, (December, 1970).

5

Parallel Bars

Parallel bars is generally the easiest of the apparatus events. The skills are frequently learned with less difficulty than skills on the high bar or the side horse. It is possible that the similarities between the basic and the advanced skills enhance the acquisition of the latter. That is, an excellent swing in the support position increases the chances of performing a stutz or even a stutz-handstand.

A combination of basic through advanced parallel bar skills are presented (many are illustrated) to facilitate the coaching process. Also, one should refer to Chapter 13 for a biomechanical analysis of selected parallel bar skills.

TRAINING FOR PARALLEL BARS

Training for parallel bars begins with a recognition of the desired skills that will ultimately be used in the formation of a routine. Then, one must study to determine the prerequisites necessary to effectively perform the selected skills. For example, a straight-straight press requires substantial shoulder and arm strength as well as hamstring and low back flexibility. Additional training hints are:

1. Shoulder and hip flexibility is necessary for both dynamic and static skills.
2. Shoulder and arm strengthening exercises are a *must*. When necessary, a gymnast should supplement his everyday training with weightlifting. This approach to gaining strength, however, must be systematic.
3. Each gymnast must learn and develop a feeling for moves requiring quick and dynamic execution such as the extension phase of the peach basket to handstand.
4. Analyze films of actual practice situations to determine undetected faults in execution. Break the routine or skill into parts and components, respectively. Practice each part or component separately until it approaches the desired perfor-

mance objective. Then, continue training until the routine or skill materializes as you desire.

5. Practice and perfect the individual skills and transitions. Only from actual confrontation with the specific skills will coordination be enhanced and subsequent continuity of performance be realized.

6. Because endurance is so important for almost all vigorous performances, the most expedient method of increasing the endurance of a specific muscle group is of prime concern. The idea of developing the endurance capacity of the upper arm and shoulder muscles to better resist fatigue and recover faster after fatigue is not a classic approach to skill acquisition. But regardless of the previous methods of a trial and error nature, it behooves the coach to use an interval training approach to increase endurance (Boone, 1975a; Boone, 1975b).

The interval training approach is designed to confront the performer with as much work as possible before the onset of fatigue. Suppose a workout on the parallel bars consists of 30 minutes and as many executions of a given routine as possible. In this case, the performance would no doubt suffer as the performer gradually reaches final exhaustion. However, it seems more fruitful for increased endurance potential to adjust the workout according to any of the following ways:

a. The intensity of the workout should be gradual. The performer should continue his warm-up and stretching and then gradually get into the swing of things. It is wrong to get on an apparatus and struggle through combinations without giving the body time to adjust and sustain the exercise rate, thus creating an "oxygen debt" that must be repaid quickly. The demand for oxygen from the circulatory system must be gradual so that the exercise can be endured for a fairly long period of time (O'Shea, 1969).

b. The duration of work on the parallel bars should at first be gradual. Hence, the duration as well as the intensity of each workout should be gradual to distribute evenly the performer's energy over the entire workout. Moreover, as the performer becomes more efficient during performance, he will also waste less energy in unnecessary movements.

c. As the performer becomes more skilled neuromuscularly, the rest interval between successive workouts on a particular apparatus should be shortened (but not too much). It is necessary to keep the overload principle in use to insure an increase in endurance, as well as to increase the performer's ability to tolerate a high level of lactic acid.

7. Lastly, but most important, *think positive, believe in yourself,* and *work hard.* You can be a gymnast if you really want to be.

PARALLEL BAR SKILLS

Swinging

The swing is from the shoulders and not from the hips. The arms must remain straight. The up swing requires a slight flexion in the hips while the back swing may experience a slight arch in the back. Too much flexion in the front swing and extension in the back swing will distract from proper execution. The shoulders should lean backward of the base to keep the center of gravity close to the hands as the legs swing forward. During the back swing, the shoulders move in front of the base of support.

Front Dismount

The name indicates that the front of the body passes over the bars. The center of gravity is kept close to the base by leaning forward (shoulders in front of the hands) as the legs swing as high as possible. At the top of the back swing where velocity is zero, the weight shifts to the left. The hand releases the bar and moves to the other bar at which time the left hand releases to permit continued displacement of the body to the side of the bar. The right hand controls the descent and balance upon landing on the mat. *Spotting:* The spotter should stand to the side where the performer is dismounting. He should grasp the performer's arm, if necessary, to help maintain balance.

Rear Dismount

The rear passes over the bars at the end of the front swing. For some reason, this vault is used more frequently by beginners than is the front dismount. It is probably because they can see the bars in front, and thus there is (in their minds) less chance of hitting the legs upon dismounting. The hand movements are similar to the front dismount except that they are behind the performer. *Spotting:* The spotter should stand on the side of the bars where the performer intends to land. Again, the performer's upper arm should be grasped if necessary for a safe landing.

Shoulder Stand

The performer must acquire a straddle seat position from which the shoulders lean forward to contact the bars. The hands do not release the bars during the lean. It is important to press the elbows toward the floor to keep the shoulders above the bars. The hips are then raised above the base, which is actually larger than when performing a headstand on the floor, and the legs are positioned above the hips. The back is generally forced to acquire a small arch to keep the center of gravity within the base. Also, for balance, the head is slightly hyperextended so that the performer can see the floor. *Spotting:* The spotter stands to the side of the performer with one hand placed on his back (to correct overbalance) and the other on his elbow (to prevent a slip between the bars). Be careful, when the bars are low, not to allow the performer's uncorrected forward displacement to injure the spotter's arm by getting it caught between the performer and the bar.

Upper-Arm Kip

On the up swing (of an upper-arm swing position), the legs are carried high above the bars to end in front of the face as the hips are flexed. The initial movement of legs up and forward (transfer of momentum) lessens the resistance to pressing downward on the bars. As a result, the action of the legs and arms raises the body to a full-support position. It is important that the arms and legs remain straight when moving from the half-support to the full-support position. *Spotting:* The spotter stands to the side of the performer. He places one hand at the back of the performer (to assist with the upward movement of the shoulders) while the other hand waits to assist the legs by supporting and preventing unnecessary motion.

Back Uprise

The back uprise, for teaching purposes, often begins by swinging from a piked upper-arm support position. The hips are forcefully extended as the shoulders move closer to the hands. At the bottom of the swing, the performer should acquire a small pike to increase the speed of the last half of the swing. As the legs and hips move above the bars (the higher the better), the finishing touch is a full extension of the arms. *Spotting:* The spotter can help by placing one hand under the chest and the other under the leg to aid the performer in acquiring the desired height.

Front Uprise

The performer begins by swinging in an upper-arm support position. He swings forward, acquiring a small pike at the bottom to minimize gravity's effects during the ascent. As the feet move closer to the base, a forceful forward and downward push with the hands elevates the body above the bars. The performer should then straighten his body (hip extension) to prevent the hips from staying too close to the base. *Spotting:* The spotting technique is similar to the one used for the upper-arm kip.

Single Leg Cut and Catch (from Swing)

During the back swing of a straight-arm support position, the performer's shoulders lean forward of the hands (the base) and particularly to the opposite side of the cutting leg. That is, when cutting the right leg, the left arm leans both laterally and forward to support and maintain balance as the right hand is released to allow forward movement of the cutting leg. As the right leg passes over the front part of the bar, both legs move together to return to a straight-arm support position. *Spotting:* The spotter should spot (in this case) on the side where the performer is leaning. Thus, the support arm (left arm) should be stabilized.

Takai (Glide Kip, Reverse Straddle Cut), Peach Basket to Handstand

The first couple of moves should be dynamic and well executed to make a good first impression. The introduction of the Takai is a relatively new move. It is impressive and difficult to execute correctly. Since the gymnast finishes the move in a front support position, the subsequent skill should logically be either a peach

Figure 5-1: Takai (Glide Kip, Reverse Straddle Cut), Peach Basket to Handstand.

basket to handstand or a cast to a straight-arm support position. (See Figure 5-1.) The main coaching hints are:

1. The Takai is a combination of two moves. The first part is actually a glide kip. The approach should be very high with the hips at least as high as the shoulders. Generally, a gymnast will slide his hands down the bars to better position himself with respect to the routine. As the shoulders descend beneath the bars, the hips must always be piked. The feet usually pass just above the mat. As the feet move in front of the hips, the body is extended by a small elevation of the hips (hyperextension). At this point, the hips are very quickly flexed and remain piked until the legs pass between the bars.

2. The reverse straddle cut commences as the legs are extended to help raise the gymnast. The continued downward pressure of the hands against the bars raises the gymnast too. The hands must release the bars while the legs are spread to pass over and behind the placement of the hands. The regrasp must be very quick to support the upper body as it aids in positioning of the legs. To insure success, the shoulders must move in front of the hands to keep the center of gravity within the base.

3. The peach basket to handstand begins with a controlled movement of the shoulders behind the base as the legs descend beneath the bars (early drop). The gymnast must pike and maintain it throughout the forward swing of the hips. As the hips approach the height of the bars, the gymnast must vigorously extend the legs vertically. The hands must remain in contact with the bars as long as possible to realize the vertical lift. The regrasp of the bars begins the upward movement to the handstand position.

Lay Away, Streuli, Cast to Upper-Arm Support

Figure 5-2:   Lay Away, Streuli, Cast to Upper-Arm Support.

The streuli is a skill requiring an excellent upper-arm swing and quick reflexes. (See Figure 5-2.) Gymnasts often shy away from this skill because it is difficult to execute correctly. However, the cast to an upper-arm support is a fairly easy skill. Basically, it is a transitional skill connecting the streuli to the Japanese Salto. The main coaching hints are:

1. The descent must be controlled. The shoulders must remain at bar level. The swing begins with a continuation of a slightly arched position.

2. The front swing, however, is piked to decrease the resistance to the vertical motion.

3. As the arms release the bars, the back is arched to enhance angular momentum.

4. The head is lifted to visually locate the bars. The hands reach for the bars to sustain the force directed downward.

5. The arms are straightened to assume the handstand position.

6. The shoulders move in front of the base as the legs descend. Once again, this is necessary to maintain dynamic balance. The same principle applies to the front swing too.

7. The hips are flexed above the bars (late drop). The pike becomes increasingly tighter as the gymnast approaches the bottom of the swing.

8. The hands must remain in contact with the bars to utilize the force derived from the forward swing and slight hip extension. Naturally, the hands must eventually release the bars to allow a repositioning of the shoulders and arms. Ideally, the legs should be above the chest upon regrasp.

Japanese Salto, Straddle Cut to "L" Support, Straight-Straight Press to Handstand

Figure 5-3: Japanese Salto, Straddle Cut to "L" Support, Straight-Straight Press to Handstand.

The front salto is an interesting skill which may be performed from a straight-arm support position or from an upper-arm support position (Japanese Salto). The latter technique would appear to be the harder of the two skills. The straddle cut to "L" support followed by a press to the handstand is a standard parallel bar combination. (See Figure 5-3.) The main coaching hints are:

1. As the legs descend beneath the bars, the body is straight to increase the effect of gravity. The up swing is made easier by arching the back. This technique reduces the resistance to the back-upward swing.

2. The arch dissipates at about bar level as the hips begin to lead the body in a definite vertical direction.

3. The gymnast pikes more vigorously, resulting in an upward displacement of the chest and shoulder area. As the hips rotate and move closer to the bars, the hands reach very quickly to stablize the forces.

4. The hips are straightened during the down and back swing. However, at the peak of the back swing, the legs straddle the bars as the hips are quickly flexed. An additional upward force is gained via the arm push and reaction of the bars.

5. As the legs move toward each other, the hands reach for the bars to control the movement (e.g., "L" support).

6. The press begins by lifting the hips and spreading the legs. These movements are aided by a forward displacement of the shoulders beyond the base of support (the hands). Once the hips are above the shoulders and the shoulders above the base, the legs should come together resulting in a handstand.

Stutz, Lay Away, Front Uprise, Front Salto (One-Half Twist)

This combination of skills is frequently used to finalize a parallel bar routine. (See Figure 5-4.) Therefore, it requires some consideration in reference to the execution of each skill as well as the integration of one skill into the next. The main coaching hints are:

1. The forward swing is characterized by hip flexion to increase the upward movement. Hence, ultimately, the one-half twist is also enhanced.

2. The twist begins in the pike position. The right hip initiates the twist action in accordance with the release of the right arm. It is very important that the left arm remains straight and in contact with the bar throughout the upward twist phase. If the hand is released too soon or should the arm bend, the height of the upward thrust will be adversely influenced.

3. As both hands regrasp the bars, the arms are flexed to allow the descent of the body (lay away) upon the bars. As the legs move in front of the supports, the hips are flexed to reduce resistance to the upward movement of the legs.

4. The feet lead the body as they are forced vertically. The arms are extended to sustain the upward motion. At the peak of the up swing, the body is straightened to increase the effect of gravity during the descent.

5. The hips are flexed very hard and fast during the back swing. At the same

Figure 5-4: Stutz, Law Away, Front Uprise, Front Salto (One-Half Twist).

time, the arms push against the bars and the head is flexed. The first movement serves to add additional vertical height while the latter enhances the mechanics of the salto.

6. The summation of forces and correctly applied mechanics result in a high pike salto above the bars. At the peak of the salto, the left shoulder is dropped to initiate the one-half twist. The head is turned in the direction of the twist. As the gymnast passes the bar to his left, he should grasp it with his left hand to insure an adequate landing.

The spotting of parallel bar skills is not as complicated as skills performed on the high bar or the rings. This is due primarily to the height factor, although an aggressive coach would probably find some method of equalizing the events.

Spotting for the glide kip-reverse straddle cut requires the spotter to be to the side of the performer as he enters into the glide kip phase. Then, he must shift immediately to a position behind the performer to aid in supporting the hips as the legs straddle the bars. Since the legs come together very quickly, the spotter must move backward quickly to keep from being hit or disturbing the performer.

The peach basket to handstand is learned without too much difficulty by placing a hand on the performer's chest and legs as he moves into the hip extension phase of the ride. The spotter should also help support the performer above the bars provided the use of mats so position the spotter.

The main problem with the execution of the streuli appears to be with the regrasps of the bars. Generally, the upward thrust is too great or not enough, which results in an overswing or a lack of sufficient angular momentum, respectively. The latter is helped by placing one hand at the mid-back and the other at the shoulder to control the descent or reposition the gymnast to the desired height. Again, the use of mats to elevate the spotter is useful. He can then help the performer as his body moves above the bars.

The cast to an upper-arm support is facilitated by placing a hand on the performer's back and legs to assist him through the ride and extension of the hips.

The Japanese Salto is more involved and thus probably requires the use of an overhead spotting belt. This technique would not interfere with the vertical-forward rotation of the hips. Subsequently, hand spotting of the lower limb upon completing the rotary motion would appear to be helpful.

One of the best methods for spotting a stutz (or a stutz-handstand) is standing to the side of the performer and reaching in above the bars to catch or quickly direct the line of direction and turn of the swing.

The front salto dismount with a one-half turn should probably be learned on the trampoline before attempting it on the bars. To spot this dismount when the performer comes off on the right side of the bar, the spotter should stand back, allowing the salto to materialize with sufficient room and then step in to stabilize the performer during the descent and landing. In this case, the performer's back and left hip should be facing the spotter, as the twist is toward the bars for regrasp of the right hand.

It is important that the spotter realizes that his job is mainly one of supplying that which the performer does not supply (correct biomechanics, force, etc.) to warrant a safe and sound execution. Some guidelines for better spotting are: (1) Stand close to the performer; (2) Anticipate the actions of the performer; (3) Know the mechanics of the skill; and (4) Don't overspot. Adherence to these suggested guides is necessary to help the performer gain confidence and correct execution technique (Maddux, 1970).

To encourage the reader to become involved in the learning process, four parallel bar skills (A—Back Salto to Handstand, B—Back Uprise Straddle-Cut to "L" Support, C—Stutz Handstand-Pirouette, and D—Black Stutz) are illustrated in Figure 5-5 for the reader to analyze. Write down the main points of concern (teaching progression and mechanics) that you, coach or gymnast, consider important.

Let's consider (A), the back salto to handstand. If the arms are thrown in the direction of the spin in preparation for the entry on the bars, does this technique

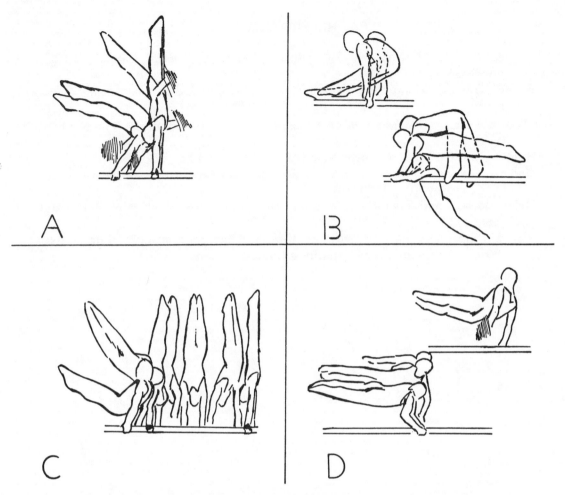

Figure 5-5: (A) Back Salto to Handstand, (B) Back Uprise Straddle Cut to "L" Support, (C) Stutz Handstand-Pirouette, (D) Back Stutz.

slow down or speed up the rotation of the trunk and legs? *Answer:* This action of the arms slows the rotation of the trunk and legs, which is obviously quite desirable since the legs must come to a stop once inverted in the handstand position. Accordingly, what is the effect of moving the arms from an overhead position to the sides in a direction completely opposite to the rotation of the body? Does the salto speed up or slow down? *Answer:* This arm action (and another technique often used in the execution of the back salto to the handstand postion) results in an increased angular velocity of the trunk and legs by reducing the resistance to angular rotation (Miller et al., 1973). Thus, realizing the mechanics involved with the two techniques, which one would you choose in teaching a back salto to the handstand?

REFERENCES

Boone, Tommy. "The Specificity of Gymnastic Training," *Gymnast*, (January, 1975a), pp. 38, 39.

Boone, Tommy. "Gymnastics Training at the Cellular Level," *Journal of Physical Education*, (May-June, 1975b), pp. 143-144.

Claus, Marshall. *A Teacher's Guide to Gymnastics.* Palo Alto, California: The National Press, 1967.

Hughes, Eric. *Gymnastics for Men.* New York: The Ronald Press Company, 1966.

Maddux, Gordon T. *Men's Gymnastics.* Pacific Palisades, California: Goodyear Publishing Company, Inc., 1970.

Miller, Doris I., and Richard C. Nelson. *Biomechanics of Sport.* Philadelphia: Lea and Febiger, 1973.

O'Shea, John P. *Scientific Principles and Methods of Strength Fitness.* Reading, Massachusetts: Addison-Wesley Publishing Company, 1969.

6

Horizontal Bar

For the observer, the horizontal (or high) bar is an exciting event to watch. For the performer, it probably represents the most daring of all gymnastic events. This is not to say that the other events are without potential injury, but rather that more risk is present when performing over eight feet above the mat. In addition, the performer must release and regrasp the bar; whereas, for example one does not release the rings at a similar height.

The high bar skills are predominantly swinging movements modified in appearance only by the performer's necessity to execute a variety of skills (in a routine). The reverse giant swing, e.g., is executed in a fully stretched position, yet the next skill may be a stoop-in dislocate to eagle, which requires a deep pike position. Both skills are swinging movements, but one skill (reverse giant) is a long swing while the other skill (stoop-in and/or forward seat circle) is a short swing. Also, a horizontal bar routine consists of traditional and variational movements composed in such a way as to enhance the quality of the routine.

TRAINING FOR HORIZONTAL BAR

Training for high bar work should begin with a thorough learning of the basic and intermediate skills such as variations in grip, back hip circle, front hip circle, drop kip, back kip, free back hip circle (streuli), underswing dismount, seat circle backward, half-pirouette, etc. on the low bar. As the inner bar work (short circles) is mastered, the bar should be raised for confrontation with both the learned inner bar work and the to-be-learned outer bar work (long circles). When necessary, an intermediate position (chest high) is often used to facilitate the acquisition of skills requiring a controlled descent, e.g., the under swing dismount, squat, stoop, and/or rear dismounts, forward seat circle shoot to dislocate, shoot to handstand, and rear vault catch, to mention a few.

A gymnast aspiring to be a great high bar performer must have excellent coordination, muscle strength and endurance (particularly the upper body musculature), and flexibility. He must be highly supple in the shoulders, the lumbar spine, and the hamstrings to effectively accomplish the advanced high bar skills.

Hence, examine the prerequisites for specific skills. Some skills require greater flexibility at specific joints or combination of joints than other skills. If a gymnast's difficulty is due to insufficient suppleness, the training problem should be corrected by engaging in slow-stretch flexibility exercises. Be specific and train the inflexible prime movers (those muscles which are most involved in the movement). The same corrective thinking applies when it is apparent that a lack of sufficient strength and/or endurance handicaps the learning process.

What about the care of the hands and training? Obviously, the high bar requires considerable use and often abuse of the hands to attain the skill level one desires. The abuse of the hands, however, is mostly related to poorly designed coaching and training procedures for high bar work. Too many coaches have their gymnasts working too long with relatively insignificant skills (giant swings). Too many gymnasts work the bar without a rest day for the palms to adapt to the stress; consequently, the undue stress predisposes the hands to wear (blisters) and tear. Naturally, such a poor adaptation hinders the learning process, and as a result, the high bar skills suffer, as well as the sport of gymnastics. Without full use of the hands, one is forced to perform with less than full capacity.

If the coach will not anticipate the problem, the avoidance of the problem lies with the gymnast. He must use good common sense and quit when it becomes evident that the hands are being abused rather than used. Certainly this is true just as the gymnast must make similar decisions with regard to execution of advanced skills (without sufficient spotters or practice). If he isn't ready (psychophysiologically), then wait. Likewise, when the hands are not ready for intense work, give them time. At first, it may be helpful to work the high bar a few minutes each day until they adapt to the stress of a full workout. An alternate training approach may entail high bar work every other day. As well, it may be wise to avoid working at great length, e.g., high bar, parallel bars, and/or rings on the same day. Regardless of the appropriate answer for you, at least anticipate and think through the problem.

The coach also should study carefully the safety precautions that are inherent in high bar training. The main safety factors are:

1. When teaching long or short swings, make certain that the gymnast has the correct grip (reverse, regular, cross, mixed, cross-mixed).

2. Always enforce the use of chalk to reduce the chances of slipping. Moveover, avoid the accumulation of too much magnesium (chalk) on the bar.

3. Learn the basic and intermediate low-high bar skills before attempting the advanced skills. The concept of logical progression must permeate the training program.

4. Always anticipate the possibility of failing to accomplish "an attempt." Spotters should always be present. They must be unfailing in their task to keep the performer uninjured. In this regard, use the appropriate mat thickness for the difficulty of the skill, just in case.

5. Teach gymnasts to understand the neurohumoral "fight and flight" reaction often experienced prior to and during competition. The coach can help in one or more of the following ways:

  A. Remove the mystery and insecuirty that accompanies the learning of new and complex skills. This can be done by the use of films or by overt demonstrations to illustrate the sequential relationship of each component of a skill. Understanding the developmental aspects of skill formation should lessen the psychological uncertainty of the initial attempts.

  B. Inform gymnasts that the nervousness that tends to overwhelm them is not always detected by others. Thus, one may feel more secure in knowing that his feelings don't show through.

  C. Encourage gymnasts to analyze their own mental uncertainites and to dwell on the optimistic outcomes. Help gymnasts to learn skills by mentally analyzing the transitional aspects of skill performance. It seems reasonable that through one's imagination and purposeful evaluation of the components of a skill, the performer's ability to execute the skill would be greatly enhanced.

  D. Encourage gymnasts to think positive and to integrate the mind and body in a belief of possibilities. It is very important to know when a gymnast is ready mentally to perform physically. The mind should be programmed, so to speak, to react in a manner that shares the physical burden of skill acquisition. A good·technique is to devise a mental blueprint consisting of the desired performance just before retiring to bed; a gymnastic goal may be programmed into the subconscious. This is a form of autosuggestion which is practiced in many sports (Boone, 1974).

HORIZONTAL BAR SKILLS

Cast

Muscular actions are necessary to initiate a cast (or to begin a swing). Assuming the performer has jumped to the bar, a small forward displacement or swing will be evident. As the body passes under the bar on the back swing, the head is slightly hyperextended (to see the bar and also to elevate the hips due to the arching of the back). Just as the forward swing occurs, the performer flexes the arms and hips to bring the center of gravity in closer to the bar. Then, the body is extended to lengthen the radius of rotation so as to maximize the effect of gravity during the downward swing (pendulum action similar to that on the bars when swinging in a straight-arm support position). The extension of the arms and hips straightens the body since the bar doesn't move (action-reaction).

Pull-Over

The performer should stand under the bar (if the bar is within reach) or just behind the bar (if a jump is necessary to reach the bar). Upon contacting the bar with the hands, the arms and hips flex to move the center of gravity to the bar. The backward motion of the head is helpful during the upward movement of the hips. However, the performer must first make a major move toward the bar before throwing the head back (otherwise the hips generally will not move to the bar). As the hips move over the bar, the arms are straightened to finish in a front-leaning rest position. Lifting the head backward aids in continuing the rotation of the body to the front-support position.

Back Hip Circle

The performer begins from a front support position in which he bends forward, allowing the arms and hips to flex slightly. Then, by pushing down against the bar and extending the hips, the body moves back and up away from the bar. This action provides the necessary distance through which linear momentum builds sufficiently upon returning to the bar to carry the performer back and around (hip circle). Thus, the linear momentum is converted to angular momentum as the legs begin to move under the bar. The chin is tucked until inverted, then the head is thrown back to increase the angular momentum and subsequent return to the front support position. It is important that the hips are not flexed before they contact the bar during the return and initiation of the rotary motion. *Spotting:* The spotter uses the same technique for spotting for both the pull-over and the back hip circle. That is, assuming the spotter is on the right side of the performer, his left hand contacts the back and the right hand should be placed on the back side of the legs. The left hand moves the hips to the bar while the right hand rotates the performer.

Front Hip Circle

It is important that the gymnast positions himself correctly before attempting this skill. For example, this skill requires the shoulders and head to be placed well out in front of the bar just before falling forward. This position maximizes the effects of gravity by presenting a larger suface area. The result is a very fast descent. Now, depending on what the performer does with this acquired force will determine the success of the attempt. Why? If the hip flexion is too early (i.e., before the shoulders reach a position in front of the bars), there will be insufficient rotary motion to carry the performer around the bar. However, flexing very quickly as the shoulders move in front of the bar (and the body is straight up to this point) will result in an additive effect of both linear (to a point) and angular momentum. *Spotting:* The spotter should stand on the side of the bar where the performer falls forward. In this way, he is better able to support the performer in case of a fall. Assuming the spotter is standing to the right side of the performer, the left hand contacts the back (to move the hips into the bar) while the right hand supports the legs.

Single-Knee Upstart

The regular grip (palms down) is used by the performer. Using a small swing, the right leg is brought up between the hands and over the bar to grip the bar with the back of the knee (flexion). This action takes place at the peak of the front swing when the hips are at their highest from the floor, and during the movement back under the bar. The left leg remains straight, and aids in getting above the bar by kicking forcefully downward and backward to move the center of gravity closer to the bar. The arms bend slightly as the shoulders move above the bar, but then straighten very quickly upon achieving the vertical position. *Spotting:* The spotter should be on the side of the performer's straight leg. In this way, by applying a down and back pressure to the straight leg, the shoulders will be forced upward and above the bar.

Back Uprise

The reader should read the description of the "cast" as discussed earlier in that the initial preparation for the back uprise involves similar mechanics. Hence, this description entails only the uprise part of the total swing. As the legs and hips move back and up, the performer should acquire a small pike to reduce the resistance to the vertical lift of the body. The major impetus for moving the body in close to the bar is the forceful downward and backward press of the arms against the bar. This action decreases the angle between the chest and the arms, which obviously moves the center of gravity in to the bar. The performer ends in a straight-arm support position. *Spotting:* The spotter should lift the performer's legs and chest as made available by the use of appropriate mats positioned to elevate the spotter.

Under Swing Dismount

From a front support position on the bar, the performer bends slightly at the arms and hips in preparation for a cast to acquire linear momentum as the hips approach the bar. However, unlike the back hip circle, the hips do not contact the bar. Instead, as the hips approach the bar, the shoulders are thrown backward to create the necessary angular momentum to continue the upward and forward motion of the legs and hips (not having realized a full circle). As the body moves further from the bar, the arms push away as the back is arched to allow the feet to move toward the floor. The head is held back to enhance the descent, due to its positive effect on the position of the back. *Spotting:* Assuming the spotter is on the left side of the performer, he would grasp the upper arm with the right hand (to prevent overspin) and support the back with the left hand.

Front Seat Circle

Using the rear support position and a reverse grip, the performer must lift his legs and move the hips back behind the bar so that the body is free of the bar (except for the grip). Then, the performer must move the shoulders forward and downward as the backs of the knees remain fairly close to the bar. The descent requires the chin to be tucked to rotate correctly. The arms must remain straight throughout the rotary motion. If they bend, then there is no way to effectively generate or use angular momentum to complete the circle. As the circle nears completion, the performer must open the hips slightly to continue rotation. The upshoot completes the circle. *Spotting:* The spotter should stand in front of the bar. Place the inside hand on the legs and the outside hand on the back.

The illustrated horizontal bar routine is composed of intermediate and advanced high bar skills. Collectively they represent the quality of skill execution desired by most gymnasts.

Reverse Upstart, Stoop-In Forward Seat Circle Shoot to Full-Twisting Turn to Vault Catch

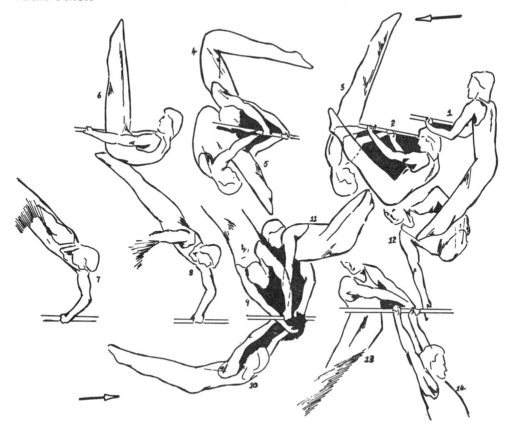

Figure 6-1:   Reverse Upstart, Stoop-In Forward Seat Circle Shoot to Full-Twisting Turn to Vault Catch.

This is an interesting mount, and it is exciting, dynamic and risky. It is composed of four skills. (See Figure 6-1.) The main coaching hints are:

1. The upstart requires a reverse grip. Prior to the flexed arm and hip position noted in Figure 6-1, a gymnast generally engages in several small preliminary underswings to achieve the necessary momentum realized.

2. Hip flexion decreases the radius of rotation, thus increasing the movement around the bar. This is helpful since gravity acts to slow the upward phase. The head is flexed. It is in a position for vertical lift rather than angular motion.

3. The extension of the hips elevates the body (transfer of momentum). However, the extension of the arms actually provides the crucial lifting force transferred to the body from the bar (action-reaction). Note the position of the head.

4. As the hips and shoulders move well above the bar, the gymnast quickly pikes (stoop-in) and positions the legs so as to pass between the arms. The forward displacement of the shoulders makes the stoop-in a little easier.

5. The more flexible the hamstrings and lower back, the deeper the pike; consequently, the greater the distance through which force (hip extension) may be applied to elevate the body. The flexed position of the head enhances angular velocity.

6. As the hips reach the height of the bar, hip extension is evident. The feet must be kept high as the body is straightened. A definite downward force by the arms against the bar coupled with the attained angular velocity generally positions the hips well above the bar.

7-8. As the body is elevated, the right hand is released and carried across the performer's chest. (This aids in the twist via the longitudial axis.) The turning of the head, hips, and legs enhances the twisting action.

9-10. The right hand must continue in motion toward and under the bar. The overgrasp grip (right hand) is more secure as the twist nears completion. Usually the left arm will remain somewhat flexed until the body descends beneath the bar.

11. The continued undergrip position of the left hand aids in keeping the gymnast relatively close to the bar during the ascent phase of the vault catch. This is done by an almost unnoticeable flexion at the shoulder, elbow, and wrist joints.

12. The overgrip position of the right hand provides the necessary vertical lift due to the forceful downward exertion of the arm against the bar. As the hips are well above the bar, the right arm also provides the final force for getting over the bar. The hips are flexed and the legs are pointed to the left side of the body. Upon release of the left arm, it is carried high above the body. This serves to elevate the left shoulder, allowing the hips to attain a greater height.

13-14. After passing over the bar, regrasp is achieved by the outstretched arms. Although the shoulders are usually parallel to the bar, the hips and legs generally need a portion of the descent phase to be straightened.

The seat circle into a dislocate full twist regrasp should be learned with the bar at chest level. Hence, as the regrasp is accomplished, the feet contact the floor (mat). At this point, the up swing to the vault position is not that important. In fact, an excellent full-twisting regrasp often dictates the outcome of the vault. When the performer is secure with the move, move the bar to the appropriate height. Now, the reverse upstart can be added to the sequence.

The vault catch can be practiced first by using high under swings (with the mixed grip) and lifting the body in the direction of the vault, but only maintaining a support position on the bar. Then, the vault should be learned out of a reverse giant swing (by changing the grip of the right hand to an overgrip). The performer should try to keep the body close to the bar during the up swing. Finally, the skill combination should be tried with a spotter on the back side of the gymnast (Figure 6-1, Step 11). At this point, the spotter can move forward to control the descent, stay where he is in case the hands tear off the bar, or move to the other side of the bar as the performer goes over the bar.

Kip (Hop Change), Forward Seat Circle Shoot to Dislocate, Russian Giant Swing

Figure 6-2:   Kip (Hop Change), Forward Seat Circle Shoot to Dislocate, Russian Giant Swing.

The main coaching hints (see Figure 6-2) are:

1-2-3. As the legs (feet) approach the bar, the gymnast must exert a downward force by the arms as controlled hip extension slides the bar up the legs to the hips. A concomitant benefit is the continued lift of the shoulders above the bar. As the shoulders reach a near vertical position, both hands release the bar, converting the overgrasp to an undergrasp. The arms straighten and push against the bar. The reactive force from the bar coupled with the increased angular momentum derived from the hip extension positions the body above the bar.

4-5. As the shoulders lean forward and the hips continue to rise, a point is reached in which the gymnast quickly stoops-in (deep hip flexion). The legs are between the arms. The head (neck) is flexed to increase angular velocity in preparation for the extension above the bar.

6-7. As the hips and legs shoot above the bar, a downward and backward pressure is exerted against the bar (by both arms) to sustain the upward shoot to the desired dislocate position. As the body stretches forward, the pull of gravity initiates the descent. At the bottom of the swing, a slight hip pike is necessary (to reduce the moment of inertia).

8-11. Upon getting fully into the up swing phase of the Russian giant swing, the hips are flexed as they tend to lead the body up and around the bar. The hips assume an even tighter pike once above the bar. This technique reduces the effect of gravity on the body as well as increasing, if not at least maintaining, angular velocity. The head is flexed toward the chest throughout the up swing. This aspect of the giant swing certainly increases the difficulty. Refer to Chapter 13 for a more thorough mechanical analysis of the Russian giant swing.

The use of mats positioned in such a way so that the spotter can contact the performer's hips and thighs will aid the learning process of the kip skill. The stoop-in is learned in much the same way as delineated with reference to Figure 6-1. However, instead of twisting, both hands remain on the bar. As the shoulders move forward, an elgrip is formed and maintained. Either an overhead spotting belt or direct hand contact is rewarding. Again, with the use of mats, a spotter can aid the performer by lifting at the shoulders (Figure 6-2, Steps 8-9).

Elgrip Giant Swing (Hop Change), Endoshoot (Reverse Stalder), Reverse (Overgrasp) Giant Swing, Half-Pirouette

The main coaching hints (see Figure 6-3) are:

1-3. The up swing is made easier as the hips are flexed to increase angular velocity. The shoulders usually approach the bar first, then the hips and legs, as is commonly the case with the reverse giant swing. The only difference between the elgrip giant and the reverse giant is the grip. The former uses an eagle grip, whereas the latter uses an undergrasp. Both swings call for an extended body during the descent to maximize the effect of gravity.

4-6. As the shoulders approach the bar and the hips and legs are continuing

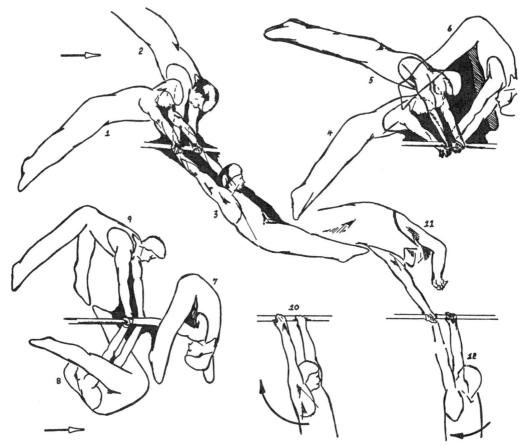

Figure 6-3:   Elgrip Giant Swing (Hop Change), Endoshoot (Reverse Stalder), Reverse (Undergrasp) Giant Swing, Half-Pirouette.

their upward lift, the elgrip is released in exchange for the undergrasp (reverse grip). The reverse grip is used to perform a reverse stalder (endoshoot). The lean of the shoulders away from the bar makes it easier for the legs to straddle the arms and miss the bar at the same time. The position of the head (flexed) encourages flexion (bending) required of the spinal column.

7-9. As the shoulders descend to the height of the bar, the straddle-pike position becomes more pronounced. Yet, the greatest impact felt while in this position is derived from the position directly beneath the bar (the point of greatest angular velocity). The up swing is characterized by lessening of the pike as the shoulders move above the bar, but the straddle position is held much longer. As the shoulders move above the axis of rotation (bar), the hips usually trail behind. As the hips reach the inverted position (where the shoulders appear somewhat motionless), the legs move together.

10-12. The fully stretched inverted position moves beyond the base to elicit the effect of gravity as it speeds the descent beneath the bar, at which time the hips are flexed to minimize the effect of gravity during the up swing. As the original inverted position is approached, the right hand releases the bar, allowing the body to turn (one-half) and regrasp in a backward giant position. The turn should be completed at the inverted position.

Probably the best way to learn elgrip giants is out of a stoop-in dislocate immediate giant with an eagle grip. A spotter can be used in front of the bar to control the descent of the performer, should he dislocate low. Also, an overhead spotting belt is possible, but not without some difficulty. With elevated mats behind the bar, a spotter could assist the gymnast as he releases the bar, regrasps and continues the movement.

An endoshoot should be learned by placing the feet on the bar and encircling the bar (sole circle). This can be done from a static position, then out of a giant swing. Supplementary flexibility exercises ease the learning process.

Staldershoot, Left Hand Overgrasp Change to Undergrasp, Cast to Back Uprise Position

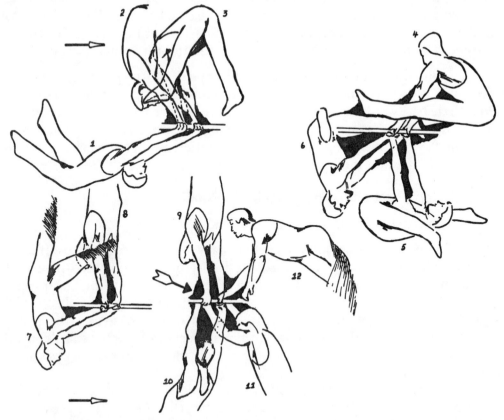

Figure 6-4: Staldershoot, Left Hand Overgrasp Change to Undergrasp, Cast to Back Uprise Position.

The main coaching hints (see Figure 6-4) are:

1-3. The up swing is characterized by a gradual flexing of the hips with the legs in the straddle position. The head is back to better see the bar. The hips should be above the shoulders, which are in front of the bar. The arm position is diagonal at first and then more vertical as the legs pass over the bar.

4. As the hips drop to the level of the bar, the arms push backward to further displace the center of gravity away from the bar. Consequently, the pull of gravity hastens the descent.

5. The hips lead the angular movement. At the bottom of the swing, angular velocity reaches its peak. In fact, due to centrifugal force (force pulling away from the bar), the legs are often forced downward around the shoulders. The head is in a natural position.

6. As the hips reach the level of the bar on the up swing, they are extended, elevating the legs. The angle between the arms and chest increases as the arms elevate the body via the axis of rotation (the bar). The head is back to encourage a vertical lift and to avoid a lift short of the handstand position.

7-12. Hip extension converts the angular movement (stalder) into a stationary movement (handstand). The arms are straight and the body is fully extended. This is not a hold position. As the inverted position is reached, the left hand (overgrasp) is quickly changed to an undergrasp as the gymnast falls in the same direction he came from. The mixed grip is used to execute the full-turn catch (pirouette).

Once again, the gymnast should learn this type of move via sole circles. Then, the feet may pass over the bar (perhaps, at chest height), yet not disrupt the straddle circle backwards around the bar. With reference to a hand spot, the main point of concern appears to be with the up swing. Hence, a spotter could stand in front of the bar in anticipation of an over- or underspin. The overhead spotting belt is probably the best method of spotting this skill.

Full-Turn Catch (Pirouette), into a Back Kip Position

The main coaching hints (see Figure 6-5) are:

1-6. The gymnast must attain the necessary vertical progress to effectively initiate the full-turn regrasp. The force derived from the extended-pike under swing, coupled with the downward exertion of the arms against the bar, properly position the gymnast. At this time and, perhaps, a little sooner, the throw of the arms and the turning of the head in the desired direction creates the twisting action. Moreover, the initial flexion and final extension of the hips facilitates the twist. Refer to Chapter 13 for a more thorough biomechanical analysis of the pirouette.

7-9. The hands regrasp the bar and the body swings forward to realize a vigorous hip flexion. The legs are drawn within the arms. As the arms press against the bar, the legs are more easily pulled into the body (action-reaction). Supple

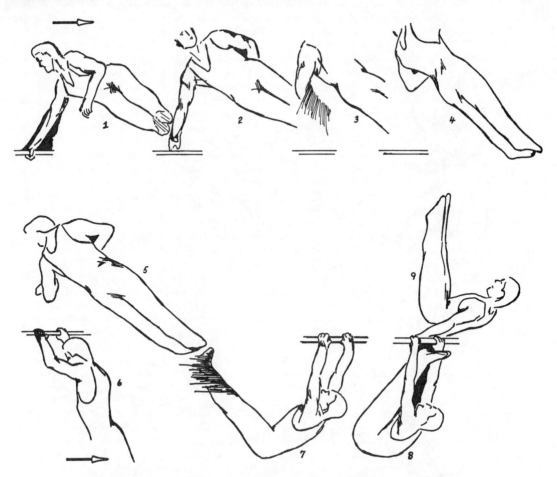

Figure 6-5: Full-Turn Catch (Pirouette), into a Back Kip Position.

hamstrings and loose shoulders are prerequisites for an effective vertical lift above the bar. At this time, the arms push downward against the bar to sustain the lift in the piked position.

The full-turn catch should be learned with an under swing back uprise to the support position on the bar. The grip is generally an overgrasp; however, a mixed grip is used too. In fact, once the gymnast masters the rise using the overgrasp, the same move is tried with the mixed grip (usually the right hand grip is an overgrasp while the left hand grip is an undergrasp when the legs turn slightly to the left). The main point of concern appears to be with the descent before the twist is complete. Therefore, when the performer turns to the left, the spotter should be on his left. In this way, as the performer nears completion (Steps 4 and 5, Figure 6-5), the spotter can reach up and grasp the performer's legs and help assist him while he reaches for the bar. The spotter is to the back side of the performer upon contacting and assisting him.

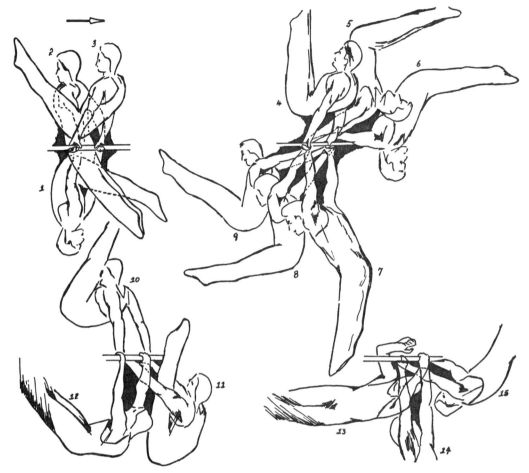

Figure 6-6:   Back Kip, German (Czech) Giant Swing, Stoop-In
Under Swing with One-Half Turn to Forward Swing
(Mixed Grip).

Back Kip, German (Czech) Giant Swing, Stoop-In Under Swing with One-Half Turn to Forward Swing (Mixed Grip)

The main coaching hints (see Figure 6-6) are:

1-4. Near the end of the downward part of the swing, the hips are forcefully extended. The shoulders begin to rise as the performer extends at the hips. As a result, the performer's center of gravity moves closer to the bar, increasing stability. From the back support position atop the bar, the arms press downward, providing the impetus for continued motion as the hips are flexed, lifting the legs vertically.

5. The hips and shoulders reach a vertical position as the arms transverse a diagonal position. The hip angle is approximately 90 degrees. The head is flexed.

6. As the shoulders reach the height of the bar, gradual hip extension is

evident. This technique maximizes the effect of gravity. Hence, angular velocity is increased.

7-15. The up swing is characterized by first a gradual and later an acute hip flexion. Naturally, the deep pike insures continuation of the movement (by increasing angular momentum). The shoulder stretch must be maintained until the hips are above the bar. Then, they move into (stoop-in) the bar as the displaced center of gravity elicits a downward motion. As the feet pass beneath the bar, the hips are extended. The under swing with a one-half turn to a forward swing results in a mixed grip. The forward swing culminates with the shoulders, hips, and legs above the high bar.

The German giant swing is usually spotted while elevated by mats beneath the high bar. The performer sits on the bar. The movement begins as the performer pulls out of an arch and elevates his hips. A spotter usually assists by placing one hand under the performer's hips and helping him acquire the right position. Also, the same spotter can place one hand on the performer's back (Steps 6, 7, 8, and 9, Figure 6-6) and help him to extend the body at the shoulder position and elevate the body during the front swing.

Reverse Kip (Hand Change), Half-Pirouette, Overgrasp Giant Swings, Double Back Flyaway Dismount

The main coaching hints (see Figure 6-7) are:

1-3. At the peak of the up swing of the hips, the right hand overgrasp is changed to an undergrasp. The reverse grip of both hands elicits the name reverse kip. As the legs (feet) move closer to the high bar, the shoulders will descend beneath the bar. Yet, as the hands are pressed downward against the bar, the shoulders will rise above the bar. At the same time, the bar slides down the performer's legs to the hips. This technique moves the center of gravity beneath the bar and then above the bar as the shoulders lean forward.

4-6. As the hips and legs assume the inverted position above the bar (or just before), the right hand is released and moves to the left to regrasp the bar (pirouette). The hands are now in an overgrasp position for an overgrasp giant swing. One complete swing is executed. The subsequent descent prepares for the dismount.

7-15. The hips are flexed beneath the bar, but both the knees and hips flex during the up swing (Step 8). This sequence results in an increased velocity and initiation of the tucking action exemplified throughout the double back flyaway dismount. One and one-half turns should be completed at least by the height of the bar. The remaining one-half turn is used for preparation for landing.

The double back flyaway dismount from the high bar or the rings should first be learned on the trampoline. Then, with the help of an overhead spotting belt, a spotter will be able to properly assist the performer. Not until the skill is performed without problems should the belt be removed. Later, hand spotting can be effec-

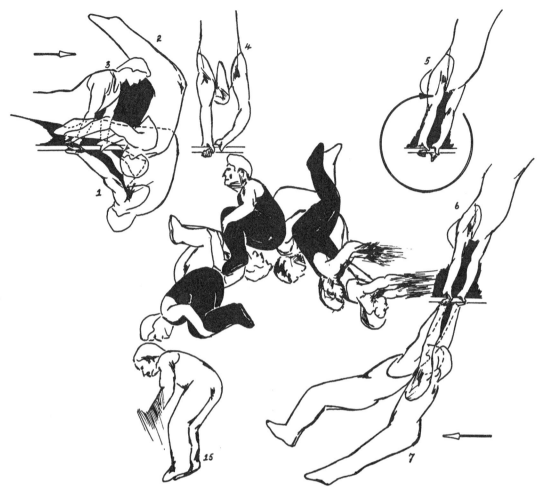

Figure 6-7:   Reverse Kip (Hand Change), Half-Pirouette, Overgrasp Giant Swings, Double Back Flyaway Dis-
mount.

tive. The spotter should be on the lookout for an overspin in which the performer
will land on his neck or upper back. Underspin is not that critical since most
gymnasts will get around to the feet. A spotter should also be alert for an early
release of the bar, resulting in too much forward travel.

In case a gymnast has some difficulty with performing the double back flyaway
(tuck position), Figure 6-8 illustrates six additional dismounts which may appeal to
the gymnast. They are: (A) double back salto, pike position; (B) double twisting
flyaway; (C) forward (inward) front flyaway with one-half twist, pike position (Barani); (D) hecht (legs together); (E) hecht (full twist); and (F) hecht (legs astride).
Analyze the basic mechanics involved in these skills. Think about how you would
teach and spot each one.

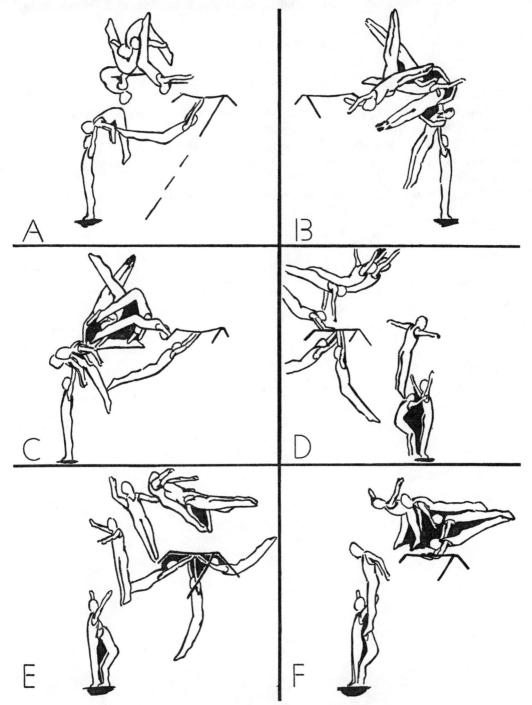

Figure 6-8: (A) Double Back Salto, Pike Position; (B) Double Twisting Flyaway; (C) Forward (inward) Front Flyaway with One-Half Twist, Pike Position; (D) Hecht (legs together); (E) Hecht (full twist); (F) Hecht (legs astride).

REFERENCES

Boone, Tommy. "Developing Confident Athletes," *Coach and Athlete,* Vol. 33, No. 5, (December, 1970).

Boone, Tommy. "Psychophysiological Concepts Applied to Gymnastic Coaching," *Florida JOHPER,* Vol. 12, No. 3, (August, 1974).

Charteris, Jack. *This Is Gymnastics.* Champaign, Illinois: Stipes Publishing Co., 1969.

Maddux, Gordon T. *Men's Gymnastics.* Pacific Palisades, California: Goodyear Publishing Company, Inc., 1970.

Stern, William. "Double Release Movements on the Horizontal Bar," *Athletic Journal,* Vol. 55, No. 4, (December 1974).

7

Rings

Most gymnasts are easily encouraged to work the rings. They like the idea of being able to perform skills such as a cross, a planche, or a streuli to handstand. Why? They look impressive and attract attention. They also require above average strength. Hence, gymnasts with noticeable muscle strength and motivation generally acquire ring skills fairly easily. That is, provided they can coordinate effectively requisite skill parts.

Coordinating swingful skills on the rings is a difficult and sometimes prolonged task. To work toward uninhibited swings is a must for gymnasts. Suppleness of the shoulders is extremely valuable and assists in coordinating the requisite parts of a skill.

TRAINING FOR RINGS

Since work on the rings requires above average strength, coordination, and flexibility, coaches must train their gymnasts accordingly. Strength training should be concerned with shoulder and arm development via dynamic (weight-lifting) and/or static (isometrics) exercises.

Naturally, it becomes necessary to use certain skills to produce strength gains in specific muscles. By placing more emphasis on certain skills, e.g., cross, handstand, swings, etc., not only will a strength gain be evident, but the skill will be executed with less resistance. As a result, coordination apparently increases as the skill is practiced correctly. In this case, strength via weight lifting would only be a supplement to ring work.

Weight lifters have above average strength, but the large percentage, if any, will not perform a cross or even a handstand in the rings. They are strong, but unable to fully utilize their strength potential. Strength is important, but neuromuscular facilitation is too. Which one is more important than the other may well depend upon the individual gymnast.

It is the coach's responsiblity to analyze and find out what it is that interferes with the acquisition of a specific skill. If the gymnast has a good swing, then consider the possibility of insufficient strength and work accordingly. On the other hand, if the gymnast is sufficiently strong to execute requisite parts of strength and swingful skills, then examine his range of motion. There may be a problem with flexibility.

Generally, however, strength is basic to performance on the rings. It is the most important single factor in learning ring skills, and thus the coach should be aware of the conditions which affect strength development. For example, training (via gymnastics) and progressive resistance (via weight lifting) will increase muscle strength. To continue an increase in strength, gymnasts must contract their muscles against heavy resistance, and the resistance must be progressively increased as the muscles adapt and become stronger. The resistance may be specific exercises such as pull-ups or dips, weight-lifting, and/or the crossmaster. The main point is that heavy resistance is the necessary stimulus to build strength.

RING SKILLS

Basket Hang

The performer is inverted, piked, and looking at his legs. The hands (palms) usually face each other. Arms and legs are straight, toes pointed. *Spotting:* Place a hand under the back and hips to help the performer acquire a comfortable, yet balanced position.

Inverted Hang

Again, the performer is inverted, but this time the body is fully extended. The position of the head depends on the performer, but is usually slightly back so as to see the floor. This position is usually used to get into a basket hang position for a subsequent extension of the legs, as when performing a dislocate. *Spotting:* The spotter is alert to a slip of a hand; thus, he generally places some support at the shoulder region and back or stomach to prevent any movement which would displace the center of gravity outside of the hands. In this case, the base is above the center of mass—now how can that be?

Muscle-Up

For the beginner, this skill often provides the only means by which he can get to a support position to practice such skills as the shoulder stand or an "L" support. To begin the upward movement, one must first get a false grip and then pull the chest up to the rings. At this point, kick the legs downward to help elevate the upper body into the rings as the hands turn outward. To finish the transition from a hang to the support position, one simply straightens the arms. *Spotting:* The spotter should stand to the side of the performer and assist him when it is evident that he can't make it.

Double Leg Cut Dismount

The performer positions himself in a piked inverted-hang position. To dismount, the performer rocks or pulls himself forward with the legs spread. As the legs are about to touch the arms, the hands release the rings, allowing continued rotary motion of the legs. As the body is straightened the feet land beneath the rings. *Spotting:* The spotter should stand behind the performer and support the hips or back as the legs rotate forward.

Back Double Leg Straddle Dismount

Generally, the preparation for this skill involves a forward swing. The performer pikes slightly at the bottom of the forward swing to hasten the up and back rotation of the legs to the rings. But instead of keeping the legs together (as one would do for the basket hang), the legs are spread so that the thighs or even the hips can contact the rings. Just as contact is made, the hands release the rings to allow the generated angular momentum to carry the performer over to his feet beneath the rings. *Spotting:* The spotter stands to the side of the performer and supports the shoulders and chest just enough to allow the feet to descend sufficiently to warrant a safe landing.

Press to Shoulder Stand

From a straight-arm support position, the performer leans forward by bending the elbows and letting the feet drop. This particular movement raises the hips, but to avoid rolling out the head must remain up. As the base (the hands) is secured by properly positioning the arms with the palms facing each other and the shoulders about ring height, the hips should be gradually extended to position the feet above the hips which must be kept within the base of support for static balance. *Spotting:* The spotter should either lower the rings or use mats to position himself so that he might help the performer keep the vertical position.

Inverted Hang, Back Uprise to Handstand

The main coaching hints (see Figure 7-1) are:

1. The illustration fails to show the pull with a straight body to the inverted position. Nevertheless, the body is straight or slightly arched as the arms press downward and forward against the rings to elevate the body. Notice that the arms are bent to increase the distance through which the body descends; consequently, angular momentum is favorably influenced.

2. As the legs descend, the arms are straightened. The rings are pushed

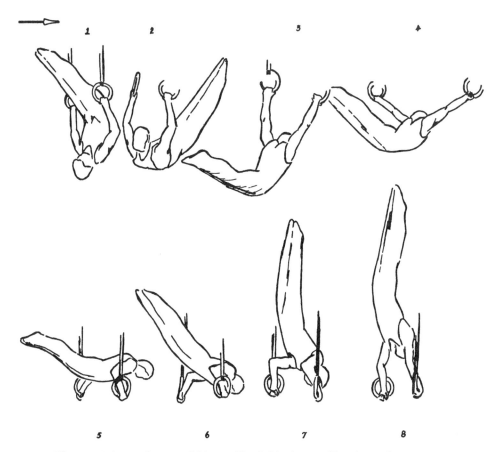

Figure 7-1:   Inverted Hang, Back Uprise to Handstand.

backward, resulting in a smoother descent. This technique also maximizes the effect of gravity on the fully stretched body.

3. As the legs pass beneath the rings, the back is arched to increase the upward swing. The head is flexed. This is in accordance with the direction of the swing.

4. As the body assumes a more horizontal position, the back is less arched. The arms move back toward the hips to aid in continuing the sequence. This also positions the hands closer to the center of gravity, resulting in increased stability.

5-8. As the body continues its flight above the rings, the arms are quickly flexed at the elbows. This technique allows the shoulders to remain relatively motionless as the hips and legs move upward. Once the legs are approximately 45 degrees, the arms are extended. They should reach full extension as the legs and hips move above the shoulders. The head is positioned close to the deltoids. The gymnast should be looking down his arms. Should he start to fall forward, the head can be raised to counteract the displaced movement of the legs. He can also turn the rings outward (laterally rotate the arms), bend the arms, and/or reposition the legs (slightly piked). Should the premature movement be backward instead, the head is dropped in adjunct with the three factors just mentioned. Refer to Chapter 13 for a biomechanical analysis of the handstand in the rings.

A spotter usually assists the gymnast during the up swing of the skill. This is easily done with elevated mats to effectively contact the performer at the stomach and thighs.

Planche, Back Kip, Back Lever

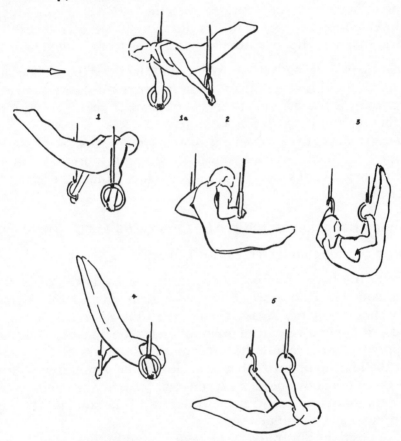

Figure 7-2: Planche, Back Kip, Back Lever.

The main coaching hints (see Figure 7-2) are:

1. The gymnast lowers with straight arms to a planche position as noted in Step 1. The arms must remain straight and generally laterally rotated. Hence, the position locks the arms. Naturally, the arms push downward with sufficient force to keep the body motionless. There should be minimum arch. Too much head extension distracts from a fully stretched body position. Also, refer to Step 1a for a front view of the planche position.

2-4. Upon entering the subsequent move, the hips descend within the rings and drop beneath the rings as the arms are quickly bent. As the arms remain bent (head flexed), the hips are more forcefully flexed and moved back-upward. The legs move between the rings as the upper body rotates backward. Hip extension is extremely fast and above the rings. The back is generally slightly arched. The rings rotate outward and support the body. The bent arm position is characteristic of the last phase of the kip.

5. The body descends beneath the rings to a back lever. The arms gradually extend in accordance with the desire to keep the body horizontal as it descends. The back lever position is held with less difficulty if the performer tightens the back and arm muscles. Hip extensors keep the hips from piking.

The planche is a strength move. Work it on the floor first. Then, use a trampoline, e.g., with the rings lower than usual, to derive the desired effect. Working with the legs apart is also helpful at first. The center of gravity moves closer to the base, reducing the resistance to the position.

To some gymnasts, the back lever is more technique than strength. This is not true with the front lever (which is obviously strength more than know-how). A spotter assists the gymnast simply by placing one hand under the leg and the other hand under the chest.

Pull to Inverted Hang, Inlocate, Kip, "L" Cross, Pull to "L" (Half-Lever)

The main coaching hints (see Figure 7-3) are:

1-3. From the back lever position, the gymnast lifts the body through an inverted position. The chin is placed on the chest to enhance the angular motion through the shoulder joints. Again, the body is fully extended during the down swing to increase angular velocity in preparation for the up swing. The hands move to a side position to help reduce the stress on the shoulders during inlocation. At the peak of the lift, the upward movement slows. The gymnast may experience a moment in which the body does not exert its full force on the hands. At this point, the head flexes in accordance with the direction of motion and the hips flex to position the legs above the upper body.

4-6. The positions illustrated in sequences 4 and 5 prepare the gymnast for the "L" cross. For example, a deep pike provides more distance through which momentum can be developed to elevate the body (transfer of momentum). As the legs thrust upward, the arms pull against the rings to raise the upper body. The shoulders must reach the height of the rings as the arms straighten. The downward push of the arms must be vigorous to maintain the horizontal position of the arms. The legs descend to a horizontal or "L" position. The hips move slightly in back of the shoulders to keep the center of gravity close to the base.

7. From the "L" cross position, the gymnast pulls out to the "L" support position. The legs remain straight and hips remain flexed. Once in the "L" support position, the back should be kept straight as possible. Remember, when in a hold position, *hold* it for the required time.

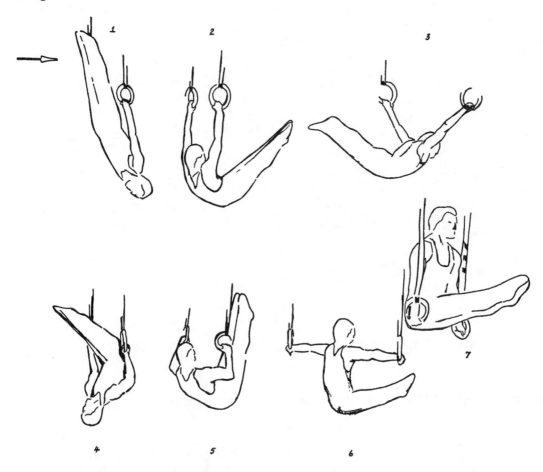

Figure 7-3: Pull to Inverted Hang, Inlocate, Kip, "L" Cross, Pull to "L" (Half-Lever).

The inlocate is learned with assistance at the chest and leg to relieve the pressure on the performer's shoulders. Naturally, the "L" cross comes after the performer has mastered the cross. The best method for acquiring the cross appears to be a combination of actual practice (with the aid of a friend) and strength training, such as with the crossmaster apparatus.

Straight Body Bent-Arm Press to Handstand

The main coaching hints (see Figure 7-4) are:

1-4. As the hips extend, the shoulders move forward and closer to the rings. The legs continue movement toward the vertical position. In their flight, the arms extend, raising the body as it comes nearer to approaching the inverted position. By the time the legs reach the straps, the arms should be fully extended. Make sure that the skill is a press and not a swing-press combination.

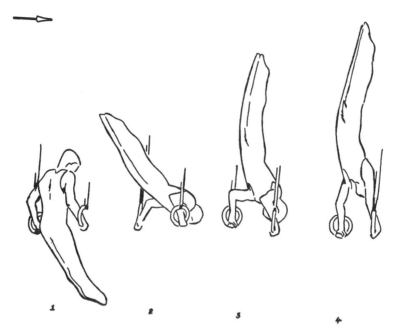

Figure 7-4:   Straight Body Bent-Arm Press to Handstand.

Lower to Inverted Hang, Dislocate, Streuli to Handstand

The main coaching hints (see Figure 7-5) are:

1-5. From the handstand position, lower the legs with straight arms. As the legs pass beneath the rings, the shoulders drop backward. The body assumes a piked position which is vigorously converted to an extension at approximately 45 to 65 degrees. The arms are straight and close to the hips (Step 3). Yet, as the legs descend, the chest is elevated to relieve the stress on the shoulders as the arms move to a side and finally a forward position.

6. The hips are flexed to facilitate the upward thrust of the legs. The head is back in accordance with angular motion. The arms are gradually beginning to bend to aid the leg thrust.

7. As the legs move upward, the back arches. This technique, like hip flexion in Step 6, increases angular velocity by reducing the resistance to motion. As the hips move closer to the rings, the arms bend and forcefully project the body vertically.

8. The sequence is finalized as the gymnast reaches the handstand position. The center of gravity must be within the base of support (the rings) to maintain static balance.

Again, a spotter can assist the performer at the chest and leg areas during the dislocate. He can help him elevate the body instead of just shooting the body backward. Generally, the shoot to the handstand is done first by shooting to the

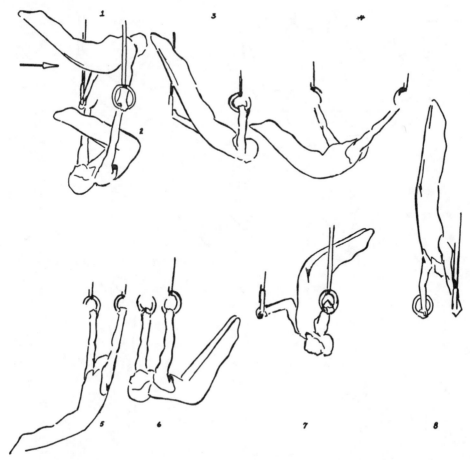

Figure 7-5:   Lower to Inverted Hang, Dislocate, Streuli to Handstand.

shoulder stand position. By continuing the extension of the arms with a forceful ascent, the movement is converted to a shoot-handstand. The upward movement must be continuous.

Fall Forward from the Handstand to a Front Salto Dismount (Pike Position)

The main coaching hints (see Figure 7-6) are:

1. The gymnast allows (with control however) the arms to move to a horizontal position while inverted. Then, he quickly drops the head, encouraging a forward displacement of the center of gravity beyond the inverted position. As a result, the hips descend in front of the rings while the arms straighten.

2-3. As the body moves into the up swing, the back arches to increase angular velocity. Yet, the body straightens to enhance an action-reaction phase. This phase is in preparation for the release and hip flexion.

4-6. After a downward press of the arms against the rings, the hips are force-

Figure 7-6:   Fall Forward from the Handstand to a Front Salto
                    Dismount (Piked Position).

fully flexed. The higher the hips, and the longer the hands remain in contact with
the rings, the higher the salto. The chest moves to the elevated legs, resulting in a
deep pike with the hands grasping the legs. As the salto nears completion, the hips
are extended for landing. The legs bend as the feet contact the mat to absorb the
impact of the landing. Then, the body is quickly straightened to finalize the
routine.

A spotter can aid the performer by simply assisting him with the up swing and
during the afterflight (or after the release of the rings) to make sure he lands
safely. Naturally, the front salto should be learned on the trampoline before attempting it on the rings.

If necessary, use the trampoline or the side horse as a static object to keep the
body under control when working on inverted pulls, planches, etc. Dynamic resistance through a full range of motion is possible with many skills and can be carried

out with a friend. An excellent friend of the gymnast interested in working the rings is the crossmaster. It is relatively cheap and has many advantages over more traditional training methods. It is easy to install and allows the use of a predetermined resistance that can be easily adjusted when necessary. One could easily supplement his ring work with such an apparatus and shorten his training period for specific skills requiring specific muscles for optimum execution.

REFERENCES

Charteris, Jack. *This Is Gymnastics*. Champaign, Illinois: Stipes Publishing Co., 1969.

Jensen, Clayne R., and Gordon W. Schultz. *Applied Kinesiology*. New York: McGraw Hill Book Company, 1970.

Maddux, Gordon T. *Men's Gymnastics*. Pacific Palisades, California: Goodyear Publishing Company, Inc., 1970.

8

Trampoline

The trampoline is generally realized to be a sport of its own rather than another gymnastic event. However, the sport of gymnastics can learn from trampoline coaches the best methods of twisting and progression for multiple flips and twists. The trampoline can be used to teach tumbling skills (back handsprings, flips), vaulting skills (hechts, handsprings, Yamashitas), and flexibility exercises to mention a few possibilities.

Although the trampoline skills illustrated in this chapter are of the intermediate and advanced status, it is certainly sound progression to expect all gymnasts to be able to perform the basic skills too.

TRAINING FOR TRAMPOLINING

Trampolining requires the participant to be flexible, and fairly fit with respect to muscular strength and endurance. It isn't necessary to train for the high degree of fitness that a gymnast has to be in. The "specificity of training" principle implies that the trampoline performer possesses a high degree of coordination, which is derived from specifically practicing trampoline skills.

Training often begins with a recognition of various body positions used when performing various skills. At first, only skills requiring the tuck position should be learned. As confidence and skill increases, the pike and later the layout position should be substituted for a greater degree of difficulty. Trampolinists also use what is called the "pucked" position in which the hips and knees are flexed, but not as tight as in the tuck position. The "free" position, which is a combination of at least two of the above mentioned positions, is used too. Both the pucked and the free positions are used when performing multiple saltos with twists (Hennessy, 1968).

Gymnasts must learn how to bounce and why bouncing at the end of the trampoline is more difficult than in the middle of the trampoline. The reaction force from the depressed bed at the end is directed toward the middle and not straight upward as is the case when bouncing in the middle of the bed.

They must realize that forward or backward rotation such as during a salto is greatly dependent upon the placement of the center of gravity. In this regard, the takeoff position influences the execution of the skill. For example, should a gymnast lean backward (which decreases the projection angle) during the takeoff, he will travel backward and not up where the action is supposed to take place.

Gymnasts should also use an editor-viewer of some type to examine a skill or skills in combination. This type of coaching and training can't help but result in positive results. Hence, by seeing exactly how a skill is performed frame by frame, a gymnast or coach will have a greater appreciation for the mechanics of a given skill.

As always, a part of any training program is the concern for safety. The trampoline is no exception. Participants must either adhere to the rules or be restricted from participating. Some of the more common safety regulations are:

1. Supervision of the trampoline is always necessary.

2. A trampoline should be locked up when not in use.

3. All performers should be appropriately dressed for trampolining, which entails either wearing gymnastic shoes or going barefoot.

4. No horseplay should be tolerated.

5. Only moderate bouncing is encouraged. The extremely high bouncing so often desired by the beginner *must not* be allowed.

6. Participants must climb up and down when mounting and dismounting the trampoline. Jumping or performing flips to the floor can be dangerous even for the experienced performer.

7. Correct spotting technique for specific skills is a *must*. No one should be allowed to spot without first getting permission from the instructor or coach in charge.

8. Avoid bouncing or repeating skills to the point of exhaustion. Accidents are more prone to occur when fatigued.

9. The trampoline must be properly secured. Mats should cover the frame around the bed, and also the floor if possible.

10. Only one person at a time should occupy the trampoline, and he must not attempt skills beyond his capacity or training at that time.

A special word of caution should be addressed to the spotting process. Regardless of the method used, the spotter must be alert and unfailing. He, too, is participating in the execution of the skill. He must quickly analyze movement patterns in often less than seconds. Remember, the objective is to prevent the performer (a human being) from getting hurt. So, don't take the job lightly—it is a serious and responsible one.

TRAMPOLINE SKILLS

Bounce

The trampoline bounce is an extremely important skill to learn and execute efficiently. Too often beginners and even so-called experienced individuals overlook the correct bouncing technique to learn other skills such as the front or back flip. This is generally a mistake. To begin with, the correct bouncing technique entails positioning the feet approximately shoulder width apart. The performer's depression of the trampoline mat projects him into the air due to the stored energy, but the legs should be straight and rigid to depress the bed maximally. The arms and shoulders are used to transfer momentum vertically. They also help maintain balance when abducted horizontally. When landing, the ankles should be flexed to avoid a loss of equilibrium. A flat-footed landing increases the area of the base, and hence the bouncing up and down is more under control. Likewise, to avoid being thrown off-balance, one should bounce near the center of the mat. It is also important to focus on an object such as the front of the trampoline while bouncing. To bounce without doing so is similar to crossing the street without first looking for passing cars.

Full Pirouette (Twisting to the Left)

Changing the direction of the bounce should be learned next. The twisting action is started as the performer leaves the mat. When twisting to the left, the shoulders, arms, and head are turned to that direction. Depending upon the magnitude of the force developed before liftoff, either a one-half or a full turn will be achieved before landing.

Tuck Jump

When bouncing up, the knees should be moved in close to the chest with the hands on the knees. This is brought about by flexing the hips and knees, which positions the performer in a tuck. It is important to keep the head and shoulders fairly erect to avoid possible forward rotation. Don't lean backward either! As the descent phase is realized, the legs should be straightened for landing.

Straddle Jump

As the performer becomes airborne, the legs should move to a straddle position. The hips should be sufficiently flexed to position the legs horizontally. Upon nearing the peak of the bounce, the arms move forward to simultaneously touch the feet (which are pointed). To avoid losing balance, the shoulders should not lean too far forward. After touching the feet, the legs return to their original position in preparation for a standing trampoline bounce.

As one might realize, these skills (bounce, change of direction, tuck jump, and the straddle jump) are generally used to evaluate the beginners. They are also useful as relatively easy skills to build confidence and courage for the intermediate skills.

Seat Drop

Using a "feet bounce," the performer leans backward slightly to reduce any resistance toward flexing the hips and positioning the legs horizontally above the trampoline mat. The descent and landing on the mat would be carried out with the legs straight. The seat, legs, hands, and heels should contact the mat simultaneously. Hands are flat (fingers pointed forward) and fairly close to the hips upon contact. The head and chest should be positioned much as one is sitting in a chair. To return to an erect position, the performer must push downward with both hands and extend the body.

Knee Drop

From the trampoline bounce, the performer lands on his knees, shins, and instep. The hips are kept straight (no flexion), head erect, and eyes fixed slightly in front of the landing. The landing is enhanced by spreading the knees apart upon landing to increase the size of the base. The arms swing upward to aid in the vertical lift from the mat. Naturally, the recoil of the bed also projects the performer vertically, i.e., provided the takeoff is from the knees and not the instep. The legs should be straightened after the performer leaves the bed to avoid traveling backward when the legs are straightened too soon. It is very important not to arch the back when landing on the knees to prevent hurting the back. If an arch is realized, one also stands a chance of passing the force on to the head and neck as in a whiplash. Therefore, if anything, have the performer execute the knee jump with a slight bend in the hips.

Doggy Drop (Hands and Knees Drop)

The performer lands on the hands and knees simultaneously. The doggy drop is often used as a lead-up to the front drop in that a straightening of the body positions the performer parallel to the bed, thus avoiding either the legs or upper trunk from contacting the bed separately. At first, the beginner should flex the hips and knees and lean forward to place the hands on the bed with the knees, as the back becomes horizontal to the trampoline itself. The arms must be straight, and the knees must have approximately a 75 to 90 degree angle between the hamstring and calf muscles. To either flex the arms or sit upon the heels when contacting the bed results in a loss of force for an effective rebound. To return to an erect position, the performer pushes forcefully against the bed with his hands, lifts the chest, and straightens the legs under his center of gravity.

Front Drop

Hennessy (1968) points out that the trampoline "is not a diving board." This is a very important point to get across to beginners. To land safely and correctly (with a fairly large surface area to help absorb the down and forward force on impact), the performer must land with his legs straight behind him, his arms flexed, palms down and fingers forward, and a rigid neck with the face forward and head up. Except for the head, everything else contacts the bed simultaneously. The skill is completed by extending the arms against the bed. This action produces the necessary up and backward rotation needed for a standing position. A safe way of entering this move is from a doggy drop. Since it is important to keep the chest low to avoid an uneven bounce and possible abrasions to the body, it is also helpful to execute a front drop from a sit drop in which the performer straddles the legs and leans forward in a stretched-out front drop position.

Back Drop

Without question, the back drop is more difficult than the seat, knee, or front drop in that one is forced to execute the skill without the opportunity to see the trampoline bed. A performer also experiences a similar difficulty when learning the front flip. Conversely, the back flip is often learned first and with less apprehension since the performer can see the mat prior to landing. The best way to start the back drop is by encouraging the performer to stand in the center of the mat, lift one leg about hip high, position the arms in front of the body, and simply fall backward to contact the bed on the back from the hips to the shoulders. The chin should be close to the chest upon landing. Also, the legs should be slightly above the chest. By extending the hips forward and downward as the bed recoils, the performer will rotate forward to a standing position. The arms swing forward to aid in the lift and rotation to the feet. Later, the performer should take off with two feet accompanied by an up and back rotation of the shoulders. The next step entails an up and back rotation of the body while first slightly arched, extended, and then piking upon nearing the bed.

Swivel Hips

Once the performer has mastered the trampoline bounce and the seat drop, he is ready to learn the swivel hips. From a seat drop position, the performer must lift the arms over the head, extend the legs down and back followed by a one-half turn to land in a second seat drop. It is important to push downward against the bed with the hands to aid in acquiring the necessary forward and upward motion of the shoulders. Then, the arms are thrown upward to continue the upward lift. As the arms are thrust outward upon nearing the peak of the vertical motion, it appears that the performer reacts by twisting at the hips as the body is extended (to bring the legs in line with the trunk). After the one-half twist is completed, the performer flexes at the hips and lands on the trampoline bed with the hands, hips, back of the thighs and legs, and heels simultaneously. For learning purposes, it is often necessary to do a seat drop with a one-half twist to a standing position several times before continuing on to another seat drop. The twist is in the hips and thus the name swivel hips. Hence, throwing the arms to a particular side will not insure success and might actually encourage worse form (in which the performer does not extend the body during the transition from the first to the second seat drop).

Back Salto (Full Twist)

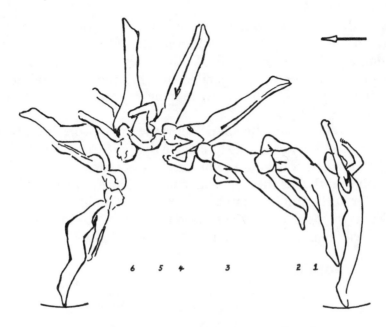

Figure 8-1: Back Salto (Full Twist).

The main coaching hints (see Figure 8-1) are:

1. The first illustrated trampoline skill is a full-twisting back salto. The skill begins by thrusting the right arm up and across the upper body to facilitate the twist from right to left.

2. An effective takeoff requires that the performer lifts the hips and legs above the base. Hence, the performer should have a slight lumbar hyperextension to keep the center of gravity relatively close to the base. This technique helps to abate the possibility of traveling.

3. The movement of the arms into the body enhances the twist. Certainly at this point in the salto, the gymnast should be able to see the bed.

4. One-half of the twist is completed at approximately a 45 degree angle. The hips and legs are above the shoulders and head. The trampoline bed is visible even though the head continues to the left. Also, at this point, the head is back.

5. The twisting motion continues as the body becomes more inverted. The arms and elbows are less flexed and more widespread to decelerate the twist. This half of the twist is facilitated by the continued upward motion of the left hip. This phase is referred to as a *barani out.*

6. The full twist is completed at the inverted position perpendicular to the trampoline bed. At this point, the hips are flexed (resulting in a shortening of the radius of rotation about the lateral axis) to increase the descent to the bed.

The best method of learning a full-twisting back salto appears to be a combination of several steps:

A. Practice the back dive with a one-half twist to a spotter while on the floor.

B. Provided one turns to the left, then he should reach for the floor as if to perform a round-off leading with the left hip to complete the twist.

C. This procedure should be speeded up until the hands fail to contact the mat (floor). The spotter aids the performer by supporting him until his hands contact the floor.

D. Then, go to the trampoline and follow the same procedure. Begin with no bounce and then a little bounce to help elevate the performer's body. By this time, the hands should not be touching the bed except perhaps to aid in standing.

E. You will find that as the performer's confidence is increased, a little extra lift by the spotter at the thigh or hip and stomach will help both the twist and the back salto. Yet, as the performer descends to the bed, a second assist by the spotter at the stomach will help correct a poor or backward flight.

Back Salto (Tuck Position)

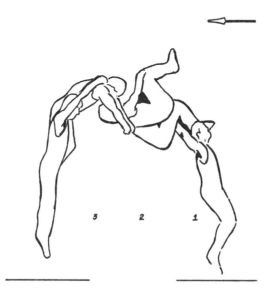

Figure 8-2:   Back Salto (Tuck Position).

The main coaching hints (see Figure 8-2) are:

1. The back salto begins with an upward thrust of both arms (transfer of momentum) as the feet exert a downward force against the bed (action-reaction).

2. At the peak of the upward motion derived basically from the depressed bed, the back is arched to aid in initiating backward angular motion. As the hips and knees are flexed, the spin increases. Angular velocity is further augmented as the hands contact the knees, resulting in a shortening of the radius of rotation. The head is generally already hyperextended. As a result, it also aids in completing the salto as well as visually locating the bed for standing purposes.

3. Upon seeing the bed, the performer should straighten the knees and hips for landing. Ideally, the arms should probably be around the chest or waist, awaiting a vigorous return above the head upon deriving the necessary force from the depressed bed.

This skill is taught without complications, generally. A reliable method involves the following:

A. Have the beginner execute a back roll-over from a tucked position after contacting the gluteal area and the feet. A small push with the feet coupled with the backward motion of the head and shoulders will flip the gymnast. Depending upon the downward force and the backward thrusts, the gymnast will land on his hands and knees, knees, or feet (perhaps in a semi-tucked position).

B. Have the gymnast practice several bounces in which he arches at the peak of the bounce. The feet should be below the hips, which should be slightly in front of the shoulders. The arms should be extended in an overhead position. The spotter should bounce with the performer. His right hand, e.g., should be placed near the lumbar region of the spine. Grasping the shorts and/or shirt is advisable. The left hand should provide the necessary spin, should the performer fail to rotate.

C. As the gymnast improves and appears ready to perform without a spot, the spotter should stand on the frame of the trampoline and offer assistance (if necessary) in preparation for landing.

Back Salto (Layout Position), Back Salto (Tuck Position)

The main coaching hints (see Figure 8-3) are:

1. The takeoff takes on an upward arched appearance. The arms are thrown overhead and then to the side (as if the body rotates through a line drawn through the arms and shoulders). The backward thrust is a little harder due to the increased resistance (layout position vs. a tuck position). However, one should realize that the acute arch tends to compensate for the extended legs by acting in a reverse way to shorten the radius of rotation. The performer should concentrate on vigorously lifting the chest and establishing the desired angular velocity (through the lateral axis) as quickly as possible.

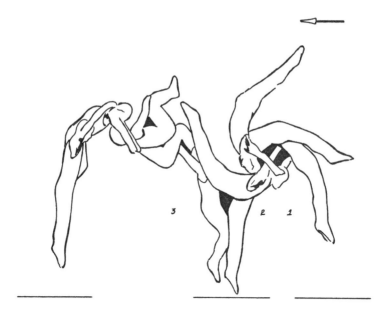

Figure 8-3:   Back Salto (Layout Position), Back Salto (Tuck Position).

2. The upper body will continue its angular motion as the legs descend to the trampoline bed. Naturally, as the hips flex to position the center of gravity over the base, the back-upward motion of the upper body will lessen.

3. As the performer rebounds from the trampoline, he executes a back salto in the tuck position. The tuck back salto is a beginner intermediate skill, but the difficulty increases when combined with another skill such as the layout back salto. Refer to numbers 1-3, Figure 8-2, for, further clarification of the mechanics involved.

The spotter should hand spot the layout back salto as he did for the tuck back salto. Generally, a more forceful upward lift is necessary as the performer vigorously arches over at the peak of the vertical bounce. He should be encouraged to throw his arms and head back-upward as the chest and hips are lifted. Upon seeing the bed, one feels that the velocity of the legs (feet) must increase (and they do). To insure that a sound landing occurs, angular velocity is increased either by acquiring a small pike or by continuing the back-upward rotation of the chest, head, and arms.

Double Back Salto (Tuck Position), Back Salto (Tuck Position)

The main coaching hints (see Figure 8-4) are:

1. As the performer returns to the bed, he must execute a double back salto. The depressed bed provides the impetus necessary for attaining the optimum height. The lift is characterized by a fast flexion of the hips and knees and a

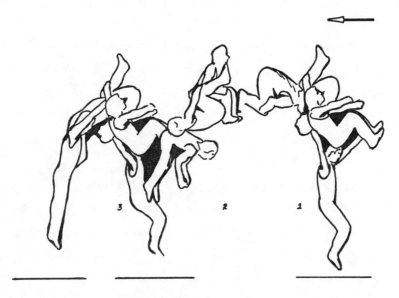

Figure 8-4:   Double Back Salto (Tuck Position), Back Salto (Tuck Position).

back-upward position of the arms. The head should also be back as the knees are grasped by the hands. Collectively, these adjustments increase angular velocity. That is, the spin is faster than when using a layout position.

2. The tuck becomes tighter as the performer enters the second salto. Upon nearing completion (three-fourths) of the second salto, the performer must prepare for landing. Preparation entails hip and leg extension as well as visual contact of the trampoline bed.

3. Upon rebounding from the trampoline, another tuck back salto is performed. One must realize, however, that it is no longer a simple skill when executed after an advanced intermediate skill such as the double back salto. Refer to numbers 1-3, Figure 8-2, for further clarification of the basic coaching mechanics.

This skill (double back salto) should be learned in a safety belt. When the skill can be performed without the aid of the belt (primarily during the recovery phase of the skill), the coach should hand spot at this point in the learning process. Naturally, the coach should anticipate an overreactive spin. An underspin is usually less complicated. In addition to the coach, spotters should be placed around the trampoline (especially in the direction of the movement).

Back Salto (Full and One-Half Twists), Front Salto (Tuck Position)

The main coaching hints (see Figure 8-5) are:

1. Refer to numbers 1-4 and Parts A-E (Figure 8-1) for clarification of coaching and training techniques.

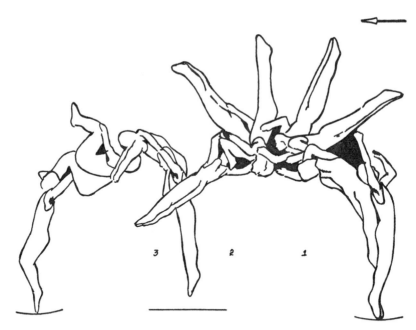

Figure 8-5:   Back Salto (Full and One-Half Twists), Front Salto
(Tuck Position).

2. Obviously, the gymnast continues the twisting action from the inverted position to the trampoline bed. Consequently, the second 90 degrees consists of a one-half twist during the descent phase to the bed. This is accomplished by continuing the movement of the left hip as the legs descend. The arms remain close to the body until such time as the additional one-half twist is near completion. Then, the arms open, stopping the twisting action through the longitudinal axis (line passing from the head through the body to the feet). Remember, twisting through this axis begins while still in contact with the bed.

3. Upon rebounding from the trampoline bed, the subsequent and final intermediate skill is relatively easy considering it is performed out of a one and one-half twist back salto. The upward thrust attained from the trampoline is characterized by an overhead position of the arms. The takeoff is almost perpendicular although the chest, head, and arms are in front of the point of departure. The hips and knees are flexed as the arms grasp the knees. As a result, angular velocity is increased. The arms do not move forward to the knees. Rather, due to the elevation of the hips, the knees are brought to approximately the same height as the arms. In this manner, the emphasis is on attaining optimum height first and angular momentum second. The hips and legs are extended when completing three-fourths of the salto. The legs must descend in such a way that the center of gravity falls within the base (the feet) upon landing. Visual contact with the bed is possible upon entering and finalizing the salto. A performer can see the bed

throughout the execution of a barani, but he should not see the trampoline during certain phases of a front salto.

To hand spot a front salto when the coach is to the left arm or side of the performer, the coach must place his right hand at the performer's left hip while the left hand is placed at the mid-back region. Hence, on the count of three, e.g., the performer would attempt the front salto. Both the performer and the spotter bounce together on the trampoline. The spotter's right hand slides inside to a more central position on the abdominal region of the gymnast. This position allows for a more efficient vertical lift, should the gymnast fail to do so. The spotter's left hand may await contact with the gymnast's back until he begins to rotate. Should the rotation be deficient, the spotter should apply the necessary force, allowing for a safe landing. Subsequently, when the coach and the gymnast are almost confident of success without a spotter, the gymnast must execute the skill by himself (although a spotter usually stands on the frame pads for possible problems). The words "almost confident" are used because sometimes a gymnast must execute a skill before he realizes that he can actually perform the skill.

In conclusion, it is important to point out that the trampoline can be used to promote and give valuable support for floor exercise, vaulting, and various skills, including dismounts from apparatus such as the parallel bars, rings, and high bar. It was pointed out in the June, 1974 issue of *Olympic Gymnastics* that the trampoline can reduce the risk of accidents when one first learns skills such as the full-twisting salto or the double salto on the trampoline, before attempting them on the floor. The number of times a gymnast can attempt a skill such as the double salto is increased and generally learned earlier on the trampoline. Hence, the gymnast's self-confidence is enhanced as he realizes that his capacity for execution is approaching the artistic status. In a subsequent issue dated September, 1974, the author also presented how the Diamidov turn can be learned on the trampoline and thus hasten the acquisition of the skill on the parallel bars. Apparently, gymnastic coaches will, in the future, become more aware of the trampoline as a tool for "sharpening of the gymnast's sense of time and orientation." But it must be used correctly (Schulz, 1974), and with considerable planning of objectives to achieve the desired results.

REFERENCES

Hay, James G. *The Biomechanics of Sports Techniques.* Englewood Cliffs, N. J.: Prentice-Hall, Inc., 1973.

Hennessy, Jeff T. *Trampolining.* Dubuque, Iowa: Wm. C. Brown Company Publishers, 1968.

Ladue, Frank, and Jim Norman. *This Is Trampolining.* Cedar Rapids, Iowa: Nissen Trampoline Company, 1959.

Schultz, Dieter. "Trampolining and Artistic Gymnastics Training," *Olympic Gymnastics,* No. 2, (June, 1974).

Schultz, Dieter. "Trampolining and Artistic Gymnastics Training," *Olympic Gymnastics,* No. 3, (September, 1974).

PART II

The Evaluation of Precompetition Performance

The importance of a judge and his contribution to gymnastics is undeniable. An accurate and responsible evaluation of gymnastics is essential for continual progress.

The gymnastic coach has a similar responsibility. He should evaluate gymnastic routines prior to competition. He should have a working knowledge of evaluation procedures and be able to apply technically acceptable rules and regulations to his gymnastic program. He should expose his gymnasts to the Code of Points, and he should have them integrate their acquisition of skills with an understanding of such factors as: (1) difficulty; (2) combination; and (3) execution.

The gymnast must learn the rules and regulations of gymnastic competition, just as it is expected that the basketball player learn the rules of basketball. Participating in an activity or sport without a knowledge of the method of evaluation deprives the performer of a critical overview of his strengths and weaknesses. In his regard, many gymnastic coaches have been remiss in their duties. They have failed to teach the Code of Points to their gymnasts.

Chapter 9 is a digest of the FIG Code of Points. It will contribute to an understanding of the evaluation process as it will be utilized in competition. Hence, it is only natural that a concerned coach would apply these same rules to precompetition performances as an effective guide to a training program. Naturally, for a more thorough interpretation of the Code of Points, coaches and gymnasts should acquire the official FIG Code of Points for Men and the Supplements and Amendments to the Code of Points (Edition 1971).

9

The Evaluation of
Precompetition
Optional Exercises

This chapter is a digest of the FIG Code of Points for precompetition purposes. The gymnastic coach should evaluate gymnastic routines prior to competition. The information contained in this chapter will serve as an effective guide for a coaching and training program. Moreover, the information can be used to inform the gymnasts as to technically acceptable rules and regulations. Once again, naturally the coach interested in a more comprehensive interpretation of evaluation procedures should acquire a copy of the official FIG Code of Points including the Supplements and Amendments to the Code of Points.

THE EVALUATION OF OPTIONAL EXERCISES

Optional exercises (parallel bars, high bar, rings, side horse, and floor exercise) are judged on three basic factors: (1) difficulty; (2) combination; and (3) execution. Special judging rules are designed for long horse vaulting.

The maximum score for an exercise is 10.00 points. This total is subject to two major divisions: (1) actual value; and (2) technically correct form and execution (4.0 points). The 6.0 points for the value of an exercise is also subject to two divisions: (1) difficulty (3.4 points); and (2) combination (2.6 points).

The evaluation process includes deductions of whole, half, or one-tenth points for severe to slight deviations from technically correct gymnastic performances (Article 17, Code of Points).

DIFFICULTY

The three types of competition (on horizontal bar, parallel bars, rings, side horse, and floor) call for the following number of parts (A, B, and C value parts) to attain the maximum score of 3.40 for difficulty. An A-part equals 0.20 points, B-part equals 0.40 points, and a C-part equals 0.60 points.

The type of competition dictates the number of A, B. and C value parts. Competition 1, e.g., requires one C-part, five B-parts, and four A-parts to attain the highest possible score (3.4 points) for difficulty. Subsequent competitions (2 and 3) require one and two parts increase respectively in the C-part and a one and two parts decrease respectively in B- and A-parts. Consequently, competition 3 contains eight value parts (Article 21, Code of Points). However, each routine in each competition must contain a minimum of 11 parts, or deductions will prevail according to Article 33, Paragraph 13 of the Code of Points.

Articles 24 and 25 of the Code of Points provide several examples of manipulating the deduction for missing parts and eventual score for difficulty. For example, upon replacing a C-part by a B-part, the deduction is 0.20 points from the 3.4 maximum possible points for difficulty—the reasoning being that the extra B-part is worth 0.40 points and the missing C-part is worth 0.60 points, creating a 0.20 points difference which is deducted from the maximum score for difficulty (3.40−0.20 = 3.20 points). In a case when the C-part is correct in number according to the type of competition and an exercise lacks the correct number of either B- or A-parts, the deduction is made on the basis of the point value awarded to the missing part. For example, if during Competition 1 an exercise has only four B-parts, the maximum score for difficulty is 3.0 points.

COMBINATION

In addition to the requirements for difficulty, each event requires specific content according to Article 30, Code of Points.

Parallel Bars

All three types of competition require that the routine consist of predominantly swinging and flight parts. In addition, the exercise must demonstrate some measure of strength via the hold parts and subsequent movements thereof. All hold parts, e.g., handstands and the "L" support, must be held for a duration of one second. Only three definite stops are permitted.

Each type of competition consists of specific regulations that must be adhered to:

Competition 1—The C-part must be a swinging part. The C-part (or a B-part) requires a lost and recatch of both grips either above or below the bars.

Competition 2—One of the two C-parts must be a swinging part. Both hands must release and recatch simultaneously as one B- or C-part is executed under and over the bars.

Competition 3—Two of the three required C-parts must be of a swinging part. Again, both hands must release and recatch simultaneously as one B- or C-part is executed under and over the bars.

Horizontal Bar

A high bar routine consists entirely of swinging parts. The performer cannot come to a pronounced stop without a deduction in points. Specific requirements for optimal combination of an exercise are: (1) utilizing the elgrip-hang; and (2) releasing and recatching the bar with both hands for continuation of the exercise.

Rings

An exercise on the rings is supposed to be executed without swinging of the rings. The routine consists of swing, stretch, and hold parts. All hold parts are held for two seconds except the "L" support (which is held for one second). Possibly the two seconds duration is due to the greater difficulty in maintaining a static balance in the rings than it is on the parallel bars on the floor. Moreover, the two seconds in a handstand position after a shoot to handstand insures the onlooker that the performer did in fact complete the skill.

Specific guidelines for the optimal combination of an exercise require that: (1) one handstand is executed with strength; (2) one handstand is achieved via a swinging part; (3) a second (additional) strength part is commensurate with the difficulty inherent in the exercise; (4) one of the two C-parts (required in Competition 2) consists of a swinging part; and (5) two of the three C-parts (required in Competition 3) consist of a swing part.

Side Horse

The side horse routine must be executed without stops. Hence, clean swings (one leg undercuts, one and both leg circles, forward and reverse scissors) must compose the exercise. Specifically, all three parts of the horse must be utilized in the execution of the exercise. Double leg circles must dominate the exercise by their inherent interwoven involvement in many of the side horse skills. Compulsory exercises must make allowance for clockwise and counterclockwise double leg circles.

Floor Exercise

The floor exercise must represent a harmonious and well-balanced execution of parts including strength, hold, balance, flips, handsprings, kips, and jumps. The entire floor exercise area should be utilized in the symmetrical and rhythmical execution of the floor exercise skills. The C-part in the three types of competition must belong to swinging parts. More specifically, Competitions 1 and 2 require one of the C-parts to belong to the swinging parts; whereas, Competition 3 requires two of the three C-parts to belong to the swinging parts. The hold parts, e.g., handstands and scales, are held for a duration of one second.

Evaluation of Combination

The evaluation of combination obviously relates to the combination (construction) of the exercise. The coach must know whether his gymnasts are executing routines according to the content requirements as specified in Article 30 of the Code of Points. These guidelines should be of a major concern to a coach during precompetition evaluation. Combination deductions are delineated in Article 33 of the Code of Points.

In reference to Competition 1, if the gymnast's routine on the parallel bars and the floor does not demonstrate that the C-part belongs to the swinging parts, the routine is subject to a 0.2 points deduction. If the exercise on the parallel bars does not demonstrate the release and recatch of a B- or C-part either under or over the bars, the routine is subject to a 0.3 points deduction. If an exercise has less than 11 value parts, the deduction is 0.2 points.

In reference to Competition 2, if the gymnast's routine on the parallel bars, rings, and floor fails to illustrate the execution of one C-part belonging to the swinging parts, the routine is subject to a 0.2 points deduction. If the performer does not execute one B- or C-part under and over the bars via the simultaneous release and recatch of both hands (grips), his routine is subject to a 0.3 points deduction for one release and up to 0.6 points deduction for no release. If the routine has less than 11 value parts, an additional deduction up to 0.3 points is appropriate.

In reference to Competition 3, two swinging C-parts of the three required C-parts must be evident during the execution of exercises on the parallel bars, rings, and floor. The performer is subject to a 0.2 points deduction when one swinging C-part is missing and 0.3 points deduction for failure to comply with the requirement for two swinging C-parts. If the performer does not execute one B- or C-part under and over the bars via the simultaneous release and recatch of both hands, his routine is subject to a 0.3 points deduction for one release and up to 0.6 points deduction for no release. Again, if the routine has less than 11 value parts, an additional deduction up to 0.4 points is appropriate.

With reference to each event and the specific requirements for optimum combination, the performer can avoid deductions or create deductions. If he fails to adhere to the content requirements per event, deductions will transpire accordingly. The information that follows highlights the negative side of the evaluation process. That is, the coach and the gymnast should determine the quality of combination prior to competition. The search for quality predisposes one to a positive approach. In this regard, mentally convert the negative statement (e.g., failure to use one part of the horse) into a positive statement (such as, utilize all three parts of the horse). However, deductions are included with the basically negative statements to emphasize the significance of positive precompetition coaching and training.

Side Horse. Upon evaluating the side horse routine prior to competition, the gymnastic coach should be aware of the following combination errors. If the performer fails to use one part of the horse, the deduction is 0.3 points. If, however, the gymnast fails to use either end of the horse, the deduction is 0.6 points. Up to 0.2 points are deducted when the performer uses one part more than the other two parts, although they were used in the execution of the exercise. If the performer fails to execute double scissors in succession, the deduction is 0.3 points. This applies when one forward and one reverse scissor is evident. However, when a forward or reverse scissor is missing, the deduction is 0.3 points. When only one scissor prevails, the deduction is 0.5 points. Finally, upon realizing that there is no scissor in the exercise, the deduction is 0.6 points.

Rings. The additional strength part must be commensurate with the difficulty of the routine. A violation of this requirement calls for a deduction of up to 0.3 points. In addition, up to 0.3 points should be deducted when a performer reaches a handstand without strength or swing.

Parallel Bars. Up to 0.3 points are deducted if the performer definitely stops more than three times. Too many hold parts distract from the flight and swinging parts, which are supposed to dominate the exercise.

Horizontal Bar. A deduction up to 0.2 points should be made each time the performer stops the exercise or utilizes strength parts. A deduction of 0.3 points is the result of leaving out either the elgrip-hang or the simultaneous release and recatch combination. Moreover, when both requirements are missing, the deduction is 0.6 points.

Floor Exercise. If the performer uses more than four steps upon entering a jump or a round-off, the deduction is up to 0.2 points (depending upon the combination and the necessity). For example, skills of great difficulty and risk would appear to require more running steps than skills of less difficulty and/or risk. If the gymnast finishes the exercise too quickly or, perhaps, prolongs the termination of the exercise based on the designated time span, the points deducted are in accordance with the total seconds either way. If, e.g., the exercise is completed or prolonged more than nine seconds before or after the designated time duration, the deduction is 0.5 points. The deduction becomes less as the performer is able to conclude the exercise at the appropriate time. Also, if the performer's legs, arms, etc. touch the floor outside of the floor exercise area while the weight is still supported within limits, the deduction is 0.1 points. However, if the wieght is supported outside the floor exercise area, the deduction is up to 0.2 points. When the performer stands, or if his entire weight regardless of the body position, is outside the floor exercise area, the deduction is 0.3 points. These rules apply in each and every case as the requirements are overlooked. Naturally, no deductions are made when the performer's arm, head, or leg is outside the floor exercise area, but not touching the floor.

Additional combination errors and corresponding deductions that a concerned gymnastic coach can effectively eradicate during precompetition evaluation of optional exercises are: (1) the execution of unnecessary movements—e.g., intermediate swings result in a deduction of 0.3 to 0.5 points; (2) the construction of B- and C-parts, which tends to distract from optimal continuity of movement skills, results in a deduction up to 0.2 points; (3) the execution of repeated parts or parts of no value result in a deduction up to 0.2 points; and (4) the similarity between the compulsories (with particular reference to the dismount) and the optional routines result in a deduction of 0.2 to 0.5 points. And, too, should both the compulsory and the optional exercises be the same, the deduction is 10.00 points or simply 0.0 points.

The maximum deduction for evaluation of the combination aspect of an exercise is 2.6 points (Article 34, Code of Points). Naturally, upon correcting potential combination errors prior to competition, the coach is able to enhance the gymnast's score for the exercise.

EXECUTION

A coach must be cognizant of execution errors just as he must understand and apply the combination rules according to the Code of Points. Hence, as one evaluates combination, he must also evaluate the effectiveness of execution of the movements. The skills may be either in a state of static balance or a state of dynamic balance. The ability of the performer to control the variables (force) altering the degree of execution corresponds with the total deductions from the maximum 4.0 points for execution of an exercise.

Evaluation of Execution

All exercises in every event are subject to execution errors. The gymnastic coach should be aware of the following deductions of common execution errors (Article 36, Code of Points). For example, deficient positioning of any segment of the body during the execution of all skills creates a deduction of up to 0.3 points. If the performer contacts any part of the apparatus with his body (except the technically correct contact of such body parts), the deduction is 0.2 to 0.5 points. Should the performer stop or hesitate during an exercise, the deduction is 0.2 to 0.5 points depending upon the difficulty of a skill or the combination of several skills. However, should the performer not hesitate as such, but specifically sit down, e.g., on the horse, the deduction is 0.5 to 0.7 points. In addition to this deduction, the coach should consider the appropriate deduction for poor form too.

Additional technical errors of execution are delineated in Article 37, Code of Points. For example, if the gymnast walks in the handstand position, the deduction is 0.1 per step for each arm up to a total deduction not to exceed 0.5 points. If the gymnast attempts to assume a handstand (hold) position that requires two or more attempts, the deduction is 0.2 to 0.5 points. Moreover, a gymnast must not use a swing to complete a strength part, e.g., an insufficient straight arm and body press on the parallel bars, nor should he use strength to facilitate a predominantly swinging part—the deduction for both errors is 0.1 to 0.3 points. A deduction of 0.2 points prevails when hold parts last at least one-half second, but not a full one second as described for the parallel bars, floor, and "L" support on the rings. Should the hold part be held at least 3 seconds over the required one second, the gymnastic coach should deduct up to 0.2 points. An arched handstand and a late recatch of the bars after a stutz are examples of up to 0.3 points deduction for each occurrence. If a gymnast fails to display correct posture upon starting and concluding an exercise, e.g., parallel bar routine, the deduction is up to 0.2 points. If the gymnast, e.g., attempts a front somersault off the bars and only touches (does not support the body) the floor with his hands, the deduction is up to 0.3 points. Up to 0.5 points is deducted for support of the body by the hands.

If the handstand on the rings is held only for 1 second when two seconds are required, the deduction is 0.4 points. If the gymnast holds the handstand more than the 2 seconds (at least 4 seconds), the deduction is up to 0.2 points. Likewise, in regard to the rings, if the gymnast bends his arms or touches the ropes (to aid static balance) while performing the handstand, the deduction is 0.2 to 0.3 points. If the gymnast bends his arms and touches the ropes simultaneously, the deduction is raised to 0.3 to 0.5 points. Should the rings (ropes) begin to swing, the deduction is up to 0.3 points. Since the swinging of the rings is a more unstable position, and the gymnast may fall without desiring to do so, the deduction for this error is up to 0.5 points. If a gymnast poorly executes strength parts, e.g., cross or inverted cross, with bent and non-horizontal arm position, the deduction is up to 0.5 points depending upon the magnitude of the error. Finally, if a gymnast attempts to swing (on the rings) prior to the exercise itself, the deduction is up to 0.3 points.

If a gymnast fails to execute a floor exercise skill or skills without a desirable degree of flexibility, amplitude, and rhythm, the deduction is up to 0.2 points. In the case where poor posture, technique, and form is prevalent without a presentation of personal (unique) style and expression, the total deduction can be up to 0.5 points.

If a gymnast restricts hip movement (impeding amplitude) during the execution of double leg circles on the side horse, the deduction is up to 0.5 points. Likewise, if a gymnast fails to raise the hips to a level of the support shoulder (during reverse or forward scissors), the deduction is up to 0.2 points each time. If a gymnast falls from an apparatus (rings, parallel bars, or high bar) and/or touches the floor (parallel bars or side horse) without losing his grip, the deduction corresponds to the difficulty of the attempted execution upon faulting. For example, a C-part requires 0.4 points deduction while a B-part requires 0.6 points deduction and an A-part requires 0.8 points deduction. Hence, the gymnast is more severely penalized when he fails to successfully execute basically simple skills. The deduction is greater when the gymnast loses his grip entirely. The C-part remains 0.4 points deduction, but the B-part increases 0.1 points and the A-part increases 0.2 points respectively (Article 38, Code of Points).

Article 54 of the Code of Points examines the evaluation process the coach can apply to precompetition training. Once again, for a more thorough examination of this topic, the coach must secure an official FIG Code of Points. The information presented can help the coach make the needed adjustments prior to actual competition. The key to excellence in competition is the prevention of unnecessary formulation of poor or technically incorrect execution habits. It is also beneficial to the gymnasts in terms of their personal recognition of correct form and style.

If the performer's hands touch the white line or center zone, the deduction is 0.5 points. He can touch the support zones at each end of the horse. In fact, the performer must touch the horse with either one hand or both hands in the execution of the vaults.

Likewise, the moment the hand or hands leave the neck of the horse, the gymnast's body position must be at least 30 degrees to avoid deduction in points. However, if the performer's body is parallel to the horse at the instant of takeoff, the deduction is 0.5 points. In cases where the gymnast's feet are very near the horse upon takeoff, the deduction is 1.0 points.

If the gymnast's body position is horizontal (or higher) as the hand or hands leave the croup of the horse, there is no deduction. If, however, the body is positioned in such a way that the feet are still at least the height of the horse upon takeoff, the deduction is only 0.5 points. When the feet are lower than the height of the horse, the deduction increases to 1.0 points.

If the gymnast's afterflight (the duration from which the hand or hands release and the stand) is less than the designated height and execution, the deduction is up to 1.0 points. If the gymnast's landing requires a small movement of the feet (hop) to increase stability, the deduction is up to 0.2 points. When several adjustments of the feet, without support of the hand or hands, are necessary, the gymnast is penalized up to 0.3 points. When the hands support the body, the deduction is 0.3 to 0.5 points. A deduction of 0.3 points is appropriate when too long of a run (more than 20 meters) is used in preparation for the takeoff and afterflight.

Any unnecessary flexion and extension of the body during the execution of vaults not requiring such movements evokes a deduction of up to 0.3 points. Furthermore, if the gymnast's arms and legs are poorly positioned, the deduction is up to 0.3 points for each deviation from correct form. This also applies to the head too. And, if these errors permeate the entire vault, the deduction is 0.4 to 1.0 points. With more drastic deviations from technically acceptable form and execution, e.g., bent arms and legs, the deduction is 0.3 to 1.0 points.

SUMMARY

The information contained in this chapter is for the coach as he may see fit to use it for precompetition purposes. It is hoped that the coach will adhere to the idea that preventing deductions for difficulty, combination, and execution prior to actual competition is a wholesome objective to attain. Naturally, the gymnast will experience similar deductions in actual competition, but they will not be out of ignorance or neglect. The coach must also inform his gymnasts as to the Code of Points so that they will become well versed in the evaluation of gymnastics.

REFERENCES

FIG (International Gymnastic Federation) Men's Technical Committee. *Code of Points,* George Gulack (translated and prepared the English edition from German). Neue Zuricker Zeitung, Zurick, 1968.

FIG (International Gymnastic Federation) Men's Technical Committee. *Supplements and Amendments to the Code of Points 1968,* George Gulack (translated and prepared the English edition from German). Neue Zuricker Zeitung, Zurick, 1971. The official FIG Code of Points for Men including the Supplements and Amendments to the Code of Points 1968 (Edition, 1971) is available through the United States Gymnastic Federation, Box 4699, Tucson, Arizona 85717 U.S.A.

PART III

The Science of Injury Prevention and Treatment of Gymnastic Injuries

The purpose of Part III is to examine and understand how to prevent, abate, and treat gymnastic injuries. Although injuries may occur regardless of the measures taken to control this aspect of coaching, it is the responsibility of both the coach and the gymnasts to assist each other in the prevention of potentially unsafe situations.

Chapter 10 highlights: (1) the necessity for allocating adequate time to injuries; (2) the responsibility of the gymnast and the coach for insuring safety in gymnastics; and (3) the application of selected biomechanical principles to prevent injuries.

Chapter 11 examines the steps in deducing the severity of an injury, the appropriate medical care procedures (as exercised by the coach and/or gymnast), and a brief overview of the treatment and kinesiology of the common gymnastic discomforts and injuries.

10

The Responsibility of the Coach and the Gymnast for Injury Prevention

The coach is generally held responsible for the safety of the participants, but prevention of injury involves the participants as well. In fact, both complement each other to create an accident-free learning environment.

Which one (the coach or the gymnast) is more responsible for safety in gymnastics? This question obviously does not have a simple answer. A number of factors must be examined such as the skill difficulty and the age level of the gymnasts before an answer becomes visible. But when one is operative without the other, it appears that the gymnast's responsibility for safety may be the more significant of the two. In view of this, a number of safety guides are indicated for the gymnast. He should seriously contemplate and incorporate these guides into his everyday practice sessions. Furthermore, the coach should discuss these guides with his gymnasts.

HOW THE GYMNAST CAN PREVENT INJURY

The gymnast's responsibility for safety is basically limited to the following guides. Each one is further subdivided to clarify specific points.

Appropriate Use of Gymnastic Equipment

Each gymnast should make sure that the gymnastic equipment is used in the appropriate manner. This will aid learning and reduce injury from misplaced equipment. The parallel bars, e.g., should not be pointed toward nor be close enough to the rings, where a gymnast may encounter upon an uncontrolled swing. If a performer falls from an apparatus, then make sure that pointed objects, misplaced mats, or anything that would potentially bring harm to the falling subject is removed from the training area. Little things which generally go unnoticed may create injury instances that could be avoided simply by periodic checking and by examining the equipment for possible defects, poor alignment, or inappropriate manipulation. All of this is to say that each gymnast must:

1. Take it upon himself to examine and test the equipment prior to its use.

2. Make sure that adequate mats (thickness and number) are placed around and within the uprights to insure a safer landing when one does fall.

3. Get rid of unnecessary equipment or extra mats which serve no useful purpose.

4. Use safe and reliable hand guards (when deemed necessary by the gymnast to use them).

5. Use chalk in adequate amounts to increase grip power.

6. Make sure that the gymnastic area is not too hot or too cold—a factor which can be compensated by sensible use of gymnastic clothing.

Positive Mental Attitudes

Each gymnast should develop a positive mental approach to gymnastics. The mind does reflect both seen and unseen factors influencing our lives. Such reflection may be via the mind as in an expression of one's personality type or via the physical as in psychophysiological diseases. The intent is to get the gymnast to function with a mental and emotional foundation well-based on a positive self-concept. If one's self-image is structured upon false beliefs, then the person may participate in such a way that his beliefs are made a reality. The gymnast who stops in the middle of a skill is probably following through with a basic belief that he cannot perform the skill. Yet the gymnast who continues the execution process represents a safer attempt (provided of course, that other factors are considered such as skill ability, strength, etc.). The best method of attacking a "stopping" problem is to educate the apprehensive individual to the underlying elements comprising the task that evokes uncertainty or fear. Moreover, each gymnast can help prevent physical injury through thoughtful mental guides by:

1. Developing a positive approach to gymnastics by coming to grips with the "real you."

2. Understanding the significance of the mind and body relationsip.

3. Responding to a gymnastic skill with the mental understanding prerequisite to executing complex skills safely.

4. Learning to utilize fear to your advantage.

5. Developing the needed self-discipline thought by many gymnasts to be the number one factor insuring success.

6. Learning and applying the rules unique to each gymnasium as perceived by

different coaches. Gymnasts must realize the extent to which they can play around for fun purposes and when it becomes dangerous to themselves and to others.

7. Not working out when under the influence of drugs.

8. Learning to relax mentally. That is, while performing, the gymnast should be thinking only about the guiding cues (kinesthetic feeling) which sharpen perception and physical performance. Relaxation may also mean concentration as well. The ability to concentrate will enhance the physical talents, resulting in full surrender to the sport of gymnastics, with less physical injury.

Good Physical Conditioning

Each gymnast should acknowledge the importance of good physical conditioning as a tool to prevent injury. A conditioning program begins with a medical examination to evaluate the physical status of the subject prior to intense physical training. A medical examination is beneficial because: (1) it helps to determine if unnoticed or undetected problems exist; and (2) if there are problems, medical supervision and advice as to training intensity and duration serves as an aid to the concerned coach and gymnast. In addition to the medical examination, the training program must develop the unique weaknesses of each gymnast. Provided, e.g., that a gymnast has ample flexibility but lacks sufficient strength to perform certain skills, his chances of injury may be very good. Conversely, a great amount of strength with poor flexibility may predispose a person to injury as well. The logical assumption is that gymnasts need an adequate level of flexibility, strength, and endurance to help reduce the possibility of injury.

Gymnastic Warm-up Procedures

A warm-up is a basic constituent of a good conditioning program. Engaging in light exercises with some stretching to increase body and muscle temperature is thought to:

1. Benefit metabolic processes. Thus, physical working capacity is increased.

2. Facilitate body movements by increasing the speed at which nerve impulses travel (Astrand and Rodahl, 1970).

3. Increase the efficiency process of reciprocal innervation. That is, the muscles contract and relax faster and more efficiently.

4. Increase the Bohr effect. Thus, more oxygen dissociates from hemoglobin.

5. Increase blood flow through active muscles by decreasing vascular bed resistance (de Vries, 1966).

The more commonly discussed reasons for doing warm-ups are: (1) the chances of muscle damage and injury appear to be much less when the muscles are not stiff or cold; and (2) there is more strength and improved efficiency to perform safely. This appears reasonable in that increased body and muscle temperature apparently supports some of the interrelated factors (1 - 5) influencing strength and muscle efficiency.

The gymnastic warm-up must not be a simple 1-2-3 number of dips or swings on the parallel bars. It should be organized, consistently performed, and cover all aspects of the body to be used. Some gymnasts typically start by: (1) swinging or just hanging on the rings; (2) light jogging; (3) stretching the neck, shoulders, back and thigh muscles; (4) loosening up the wrists and ankles; and finally (5) by engaging in light to moderate to vigorous tumbling. The time invested is generally around 20 to 30 minutes, sometimes longer or shorter, depending on the individual variations among gymnasts. The aforementioned stretching procedures are "specific" or related warm-up procedures as opposed to an unrelated warm-up in which the gymnast e.g., trains for aerobic development prior to a gymnastic workout. Gymnastically speaking, specific stretching exercises may be more beneficial for at least three reasons: (1) related warm-ups permit the athlete to engage in similar execution of skills, if not the same skill, which supplements and reinforces regular practice sessions; (2) related warm-ups usually engage the necessary mental commitment or concentration needed for a cohesive relationship of the mind and body; and (3) related warm-ups utilize rather extensive stretching, which enhances body suppleness. Moreover, upon beginning actual practice, e.g., on the rings, additional warming-up is beneficial because: (1) the performer has the opportunity to address himself to the unique cues inherent in the skills performed on the rings; (2) it allows additional time to elicit appropriate neural responses for successful execution; and (3) the performer can then integrate the necessary mental attitude with the expectant physical performance.

WHAT IS THE COACH'S RESPONSIBLITY FOR INJURY PREVENTION?

The coach is held responsible for injuries in gymnastics even when an injury may have been precipitated by an overanxious, uncautious gymnast. It is hoped that both will work together with combined efforts, but the coach is technically in charge and is responsible for his gymnasts.

Acknowledge the Possibility of Danger

Without hesitation, the coach must acknowledge the inevitable danger inherent in athletics. He must realize that although he tries very hard to prevent physical injury, the possibility is very real that it may occur regardless of combined efforts.

Avoid Working Out When Fatigued

Encourage the gymnasts to not overextend themselves when fatigued. Instruct them of their responsibility, as delineated earlier in reference to the equipment, mental attitude, and physical conditioning.

Project Positive Mental Guides

Interject positive statements and remarks to reinforce the gymnast's self-concept. Such behavior will help to reassure the gymnast that his work is coming along satisfactorily. Likewise, when necessary, it may be productive to "tell it like it is" if the gymnast is playing around. A frank gesture from the coach may be enough to encourage a change.

Appreciation for Kinesthetic Cues

A coach should teach for the general feeling of skills. Integrated with this technique is an appreciation for correct mechanical analysis of skills. It is imperative that the gymnast not only be able to perform a handstand, but that he also knows where his legs are positioned. For example, are they arched, bent, or straight? Are the shoulders extended? Are the feet pointed and together? Without the ability to sense proper body position, a gymnast is more prone to injury than one who utilizes this technique to control and maintain proper movements. The coach should help the gymnast utilize this factor for safety reasons.

Perform Without Tension

Remove tension and unnecessary physical exertion by relaxing while performing. Relaxation does not mean to give in and let go, but to control more critically the movements of the body and limbs by not tensing up and restricting desirable movements. Learn to exert a maximum effort in a relaxed manner. Surely this technique will insure safety and abate injury.

Recognize Individual Differences

Be cautious of expecting every gymnast to perform all skills. When it comes to learning physical and mental tasks, there are unique differences among athletes that should not be overlooked. For example, a standard approach to teaching a specific skill one way may be alright for the majority, but in some instances a particular person may warrant a different approach to enhance learning and safety.

Effective Spotting

A major responsibility of the coach is to take time out to teach his gymnasts how to spot effectively. Since they will be spotting each other with most skills, they need to realize the responsibility involved. Inexperienced gymnasts should learn to spot by spotting with experienced spotters. The coach can help by: (1) demonstrating and explaining the hand transfer technique appropriate for most skills; (2) introducing the gymnasts to slides, books, and films illustrating correct spotting techniques; and (3) using the rope, belt, and other spotting devices as a way of demonstrating their purpose and application.

Teach Progression

The gymnastic coach must teach skills in a logical and progressive manner. Upon learning the basic techniques first, the gymnast will have a sufficient foundation to absorb the minor corrections. However, without the prerequisites, the coach is asking for trouble (sprains, strains, dislocations, etc.).

Appropriate Use of Medical Resources

Finally, when a gymnast is injured, examine the injury and determine to the best of your knowledge the extent of damage. Then, refer him to a medical doctor or a team trainer if the injury appears extensive. Keep close observations in instances where the injury involves the head, neck, and spinal column. Do not allow gymnasts to perform when they are injured even if it means the championship. See that they get proper medical treatment and if necessary, rehabilitation. Only after the injured gymnast is completely rehabilitated should he be allowed to resume intense workouts. If an injury, on the other hand, is not too extensive, then he should probably continue his conditioning (strength, endurance, and flexibility). Furthermore, this may be a time in which skills are analyzed and routines are formulated.

APPLICATION OF BIOMECHANICAL PRINCIPLES TO PREVENT INJURIES

An application of kinesiology and biomechanics to the study of gymnastics should help to prevent injury since many injuries are often due to poor application of these principles. Basically, the mechanics of a given performance should parallel the mental expectation and concept of the movement. Unfortunately, one often perceives the skill as being performed one way while correct body mechanics dictate a different way. The coach should help the two (the gymnast and the biomechanical principles) come closer together in an effort to reduce injury and improve performance.

Safety Principles Relative to Continuity of Motion

A tumbler exerts force against the floor, overcoming inertia, followed by a series of back handsprings finalized by a layout back flip. The approach and sequence is indicative of translatory (linear) motion while the back flip illustrates rotary motion. Both types are combined and each must complement the other to insure the performer's safety.

Once the gymnast executes the round-off and the first back handspring, each succeeding handspring will either gain or lose in speed and effectiveness, depending upon the continuity of motions. The gymnast must not hesitate between each skill, otherwise the summation of forces will be lost. Consequently, the lack of continuity predisposes one to: (1) wrist strains and shoulder injury due to undue stress and tension; and (2) a loss of force needed for the vertical lift to properly execute the back flip. Moreover, the loss of acceleration coupled with increased resistance results in jerky, uncontrolled body movements.

Safety Principles Relative to Transfer of Momentum

A gymnast transfers momentum when he throws his arms up just prior to leaving the floor upon execution of a front flip. Once the arms are thrust forward or backward, the body tends to follow with greater momentum. Likewise, the execution of a peach basket to support on the parallel bars requires a transfer of momentum to aid in the execution. But, to transfer momentum in an efficient and safe manner, the performer must initiate the lift and hip extension while still in contact with the bars. Otherwise, no transfer or change in momentum will occur and the performer's safety may be threatened. Interesting results may be realized provided biomechanic principles are applied.

Safety Principles Relative to Acceleration, Optimal Acceleration, and Efficiency

Extending the discussion of the peach basket to the handstand position creates additional problems. The performer may find himself either on the floor (failed to get high enough to regrasp) or in a shoulder stand position if the components (lift, pike-drop ride, and hip extension followed by maintaining hand contact as long as possible) are not sequentially utilized. By increasing the force via either a more forceful muscle contraction, a higher initial start (lift), a tighter pike, a longer ride interval, or a more explosive extension, the gymnast may gain the optimal increase in speed to attain the desired height and execution. The acceleration must be optimal or suffer the loss in efficiency, energy, and safety.

Safety Principles Relative to Angular Speed

The common practice of tucking helps to insure completion of a front flip or basically any rotational movement. Shortening the radius of rotation increases the speed of rotation. A gymnast may safely compensate for not enough height by tucking. Thus, increased angular speed allows the feet to contact the floor in a shorter time, whereas the piked position requires greater force input and transfer of momentum to match the angular speed realized in the tucked position. Thus, as the radius lengthens, the rotation becomes slower. The main problem, however, lies in too much angular speed as opposed to too little.

Safety Principles Relative to Dissipation of Forces

The dissipation or reduction of forces or momentum prior to and upon contact with the floor is crucially important for obvious safety reasons. Reduction in momentum may begin upon descent—e.g., a front flip off the parallel bars utilizes a regrasp on one bar prior to contact with the mat. This technique increases the control and reduces injuries by manipulating (slowing) the angular momentum and speed of descent. In addition, the landing (bent knees) absorbs and distributes the force so that no one specific area must absorb all the force.

However, if the gymnast fails to grasp the bar and overturns the flip, he can still dissipate the force and land safely. Since the gymnast cannot dissipate the force prior to contacting the floor, he must distribute the force over a larger area. For example, upon contacting the floor, he should: (1) convert extended arms and legs into a semi-extended or flexed position to help absorb the force; and (2) continue the somersault action by dropping the shoulder (shoulder roll) to help spread the force over a larger area (the total body rather than an arm or the neck).

Safety Principles Relative to Static Equilibrium

A handstand in the rings is a rather difficult skill for the beginning gymnast. He must learn to control variables that distract from static control (balance) and stability. Instability results when body parts move away from the center of gravity, pulling it outside of the base of support (the hands). The answer is obvious and yet difficult to learn. The center of gravity must stay within the base to maintain static equilibrium and possibly to prevent injury.

No doubt you have seen gymnasts press their arms against the straps, holding the rings. This technique increases stability because it creates a larger base. It is not a desirable practice, but it is possibly beneficial for a short period of time. An additional aid to increase stability is the use of ample chalk to prevent slippage. Finally, the static skills, e.g., handstands with one or two arms, should be performed with a straight body (extended shoulder region, no lumbar arch, straight arms and legs, and pointed toes) to reduce the expenditure of energy. The more energy used in a wasteful manner, the greater chance of promoting an injury. Energy serves not only the function of producing movement, but is the key to controlling movement as well.

REFERENCES

Astrand, Per-Olaf, and Kaare Rodahl. *Textbook of Work Physiology*. New York: McGraw-Hill Book Company, 1970.

Boone, Tommy. "Peach Basket to Handstand," *Athletic Journal*, Vol. 51, No. 3, 9, (November, 1970), pp. 52-54.

Boone, Tommy. "Hints for Better Gymnastic Performance," *The Coaching Clinic*, Englewood Cliffs, New Jersey: Prentice-Hall, Inc., July 1971.

Bunn, John W. *Scientific Principles of Coaching*. Englewood Cliffs, New Jersey: Prentice-Hall, Inc., 1955.

Cooper, John M., and Ruth B. Glassow. *Kinesiology*. Saint Louis: The C. V. Mosby Company, 1968.

de Vries, Herbert A. *Physiology of Exercise*. Dubuque, Iowa: Wm. C. Brown Company Publishers, 1966.

Jacobson, Edmund. *You Must Relax*. New York: McGraw-Hill Book Company, Inc., 1962.

Jensen, Clayne R., and Gordon W. Schultz. *Applied Kinesiology*. New York: McGraw-Hill Book Company, 1970.

Rathbone, Josephine L. *Relaxation*. Philadelphia: Lea and Febiger, 1969.

Ryan, Allan J. "The Physician and Exercise Physiology," Ch. 11 in *Exercise Physiology*, Harold B. Falls (Ed.). New York: Academic Press, 1968.

11

Care and Treatment of Gymnastic Injuries

This discussion of the care and treatment of gymnastic injuries is not intended to cover the whole gamut of injuries normally examined in handbooks and texts for trainers. It is primarily a concise presentation of the more commonly observed injuries in gymnastics.

The primary purpose of this chapter is to discuss and illustrate: (1) the importance of prompt diagnostic evaluation; and (2) the emergency medical care, procedures, and rehabilitation of injuries. A secondary purpose is the descriptive, detailed analysis of injuries. It is felt that a knowledge of musculoskeletal anatomy is essential for a thorough understanding of sports injuries.

PROMPT DIAGNOSTIC EVALUATION

The lack of injuries in gymnastics, when compared to football, etc., has created at times a false sense of security in which the coaches are not psychologically prepared for injuries nor would they generally know what to do should an accident occur. It is believed that the information contained in this section will help the gymnastic coach to cope with handling an injury situation.

The coach is responsible for two diagnostic steps. They are: (1) to obtain a record of what happened, followed by a more complete investigation; and (2) to implement early diagnostic procedures.

Injury Record and Investigation

A history of an injury is essentially the same as a record, story, or narrative. The coach must find out what happened, how it happened, and why it happened to the best of his ability. Once he realizes the events leading up to the accident, the severity and complications are more easily analyzed.

Dayton (1965) points out that if possible the athlete should be asked to describe the conditons that led up to and resulted in the injury. In other words, was he on the rings, bars, or was he tumbling? Was there a noise (fracture) upon landing? Is there pain? If so, where? How severe is it? The recording of the events is a critical and revealing process and should enhance the investigation that seeks to further clarify the extent of damage. For example, it was recorded that Mike fell from the rings while attempting a dislocate. Upon investigating the arm which he had landed on, Mike indicated that it was hurting. The investigation proved that it was deformed and possibly fractured. Palpation of the injured area confirmed that it was fractured.

Early Diagnostic Follow-up

Ryan (1968) states that injuries such as sprains, fractures, and dislocations of the arms and legs should be treated with the application of cold followed by a splint (support). The cold application helps to control swelling and pain while the splint provides a means of preventing further internal injury. Then the coach should proceed to take the gymnast to the doctor or a hospital for a more comprehensive examination.

In the case of more serious injuries such as to the vertebrae and spinal cord, to move the gymnast would be *unwise*. Do not make a hasty investigation; do not move the injured person. Rather, send for a doctor immediately. The subsequent sections in this chapter should help clarify when to move and when not to move an injured person, and early diagnostic measures.

EMERGENCY MEDICAL CARE, REHABILITATION, AND KINESIOLOGICAL APPLICATION TO GYMNASTIC INJURIES

To help the coach be a more responsible person and coach, this section includes basic medical care, rehabilitation procedures, and kinesiological applications relative to strains, sprains, dislocations, and fractures. These injuries involve muscles, ligaments, tendons, joints, and bones.

STRAINS

A good definition of a strain is a musculotendinous rupture with acute pain accompanied by capillary damage, tissue bleeding, scarring, and incapacitation.

The damage depends upon the severity of the exertion and the inappropriate interplay between the agonists and the antagonistic muscles.

Examples of Selected Musculotendinous Sites for Strains

Arm Muscle Strains. Figure 11-1 is a posterior view of a gymnast performing the regular cross. It illustrates possible musculotendinous sites where strains may occur. The triceps (long head), e.g., arises from the infraglenoid process of the scapula and inserts (all three heads) into the olecranon process of the ulnar. The triceps extend the forearm and, in this case, they must keep the forearm completely extended and the arm forcefully adducted. Without an adequate warm-up, the extreme exertion could produce a strain in the long head where the muscle fibers rupture, bleed, and create pain.

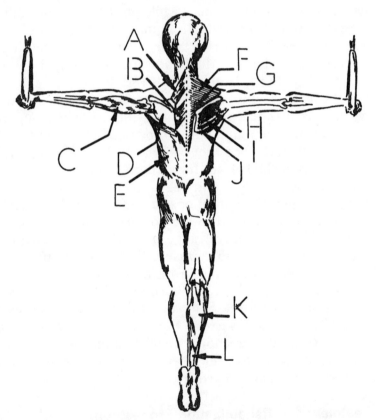

Figure 11-1: Selected Musculotendinous Sites for Possible Strains While Performing the Regular Cross. A—Levator Scapulae; B—Rhomboideus; C—Triceps; D—Scapula; E—Latissimus Dorsi; F—Trapezius; G—Supraspinatus; H—Infraspinatus; I—Teres Minor; J—Teres Major; K—Gastrocnemius; and L—Achille's Tendon.

Shoulder Muscle Strains. Damage to the shoulder muscles is quite possible as well. The supraspinatus, infraspinatus, and teres minor arise from the posterior aspect of the scapula and insert on tubercles on the head of the humerus. The teres major arises from the axillary border of the scapula and inserts into the medial lip of the bicipital groove of the humerus. These muscles strengthen the shoulder joint. Since they (except the supraspinatus) adduct (move the arm to the mid-portion of the body) the arm, they are powerfully contracted during this skill. Hence, without a proper warm-up, any one of these muscles may be injured.

Back and Neck Muscle Strains. The rhomboideus major and minor as well as the trapezius adducts the scapula. Thus, they may be injured in a combined effort to keep the scapula in its proper position. Inefficient interaction between these muscles and forces which tend to abduct the scapula may result in a rupture (tear) of the muscle under the greatest stress.

Achille's Tendon Strain. Not of importance while on the rings, but during tumbling or upon recovering from very high dismounts the possibility of injuring the Archille's tendon is a good one. Briefly, the gastrocnemius originates from the posterior supracondylar surfaces of the femur and inserts by the Achille's tendon into the back of the heel bone. If an ankle is relaxed, but forcefully dorsiflexed upon contacting the mat, a rupture of the tendon is possible. To guard against this type of injury, the coach should instruct his gymnasts to thoroughly stretch the Achille's tendon while warming up. This can be done by placing the hands on an apparatus and gradually inch each foot backwards. Keep the leg straight and the foot flat on the floor. As the body leans forward, the tendon will be stretched. Stop when the heel raises from the floor and begin again (Cailliet, 1968).

In the case of an apparent partial or complete Achille's tendon rupture, the coach must get the injured gymnast to the doctor. A complete rupture will allow the ankle to dorsiflex beyond normal range, since the anterior leg muscles are no longer opposed. Moreover, the calf muscle will retract resulting in a gap in the tendon area. Cailliet (1968) points out in his book *Foot and Ankle Pain* that most Achille's tendon tears are complete. The incomplete tear and certainly the complete tear are surgically corrected. Since the time interval between the tear and surgical intervention influences success, the sooner the treatment is begun the more successful the surgical corrections. Rehabilitation is a slow process. In time, progressive exercises designed to strengthen and stretch the injured area will promote a rapid return to gymnastic participation.

Immediate Treatment and Rehabilitation Procedures for Musculotendinous Strains

The immediate treatment for muscle and tendon strains is the application of cold packs to abate the tissue bleeding. Then, bandages (strapping) should be used to compress the injured area to take the tension off the injured muscle or tendon. The gymnast must discontinue the use of the strained muscle and allow the disrupted fibers to heal properly. However, other exercises which do not require the use of the injured area should probably be continued to maintain their functional ability.

Rehabilitative procedures actually begin with those already discussed followed by the use of: (1) infrared heat; (2) whirlpool treatments; and (3) gentle muscle manipulation.

SPRAINS AND DISLOCATIONS

The second most frequent injury is a sprain. This is an injury to the ligaments which strengthen joints. It may not take more than a wrong step on a misplaced mat to sprain an ankle.

Most ligaments are fibrous tissues made of collagenous fibers which serve to keep a joint from going beyond its normal range of movement. However, undue stretching of the ligaments causes tissue damage with immediate pain and tissue bleeding. The ligaments have sensory nerves which transmit the damage to the brain, which in turn interprets it as pain (Berger, 1964).

The joints susceptible to injury in gymnastics are the: (1) ankle; (2) knee; (3) lumbar vertebrae; (4) shoulder; (5) elbow; and (6) wrist.

Ankle Sprains

Musculoskeletal Anatomy and Predisposing Factors. This type of injury usually involves a force that turns the foot outward (inversion). Thus, one or more ligaments on the lateral side of the ankle will weaken and tear. Figure 11-2 depicts several supporting ligaments and articulating structures of the left ankle.

Laterally, the fibula is secured to the talus and calcaneus by the anterior and posterior talofibular and the calcaneofibular ligaments. These ligaments are so strong that when they are placed under great pressure, the end of the fibula will frequently break before ligamentum damage occurs. Figures 11-3a and 3b illustrate the medial and posterior ligamentous support. They are susceptible to injury too.

Treatment for Ankle Sprains. Immediate application of ice cold compresses is necessary to control the hemorrhage. Adhesive strapping or elastic bandages will also help control the swelling. Although with mild ankle sprains some athletes continue practicing as if the problem will correct itself, the extra tension may further complicate the injury and prolong recovery. Only when the swelling is down should the athlete begin to place weight on the foot. Again, the ankle should be adequately supported by adhesive strapping.

With more severe sprains, the use of crutches may be necessary. The doctor will indicate if he feels walking or other forms of activity will impede the control of bleeding as well as postponing repair and recovery. Dayton advocates elevating the injured leg. He points out that gravity will hasten the removal of tissue bleeding and hasten recovery.

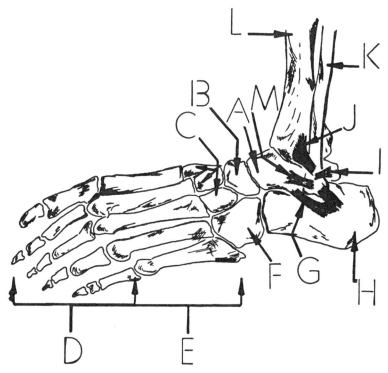

Figure 11-2: Lateral View of the Foot and Ankle Joint. A—Talus; B—Navicular; C—Cuneiforms; D—Phalanges; E—Metatarsals; F—Cuboid; G—Calcaneofibular Ligament; H—Calcaneus; I—Posterior Talofibular Ligament; J—Anterior Tibiofibular Ligament; K—Fibula; L—Tibia; and M—Anterior Talofibular Ligament.

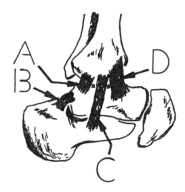

Figure 11-3a: Medial View of the Ankle Joint. A—Posterior Talotibia Ligament; B—Posterior Talocalcaneal Ligament; C—Calcaneotibial Ligament; and D—Deltoid Ligament.

Figure 11-3b: Posterior View of the Ankle Joint. E—Posterior Talofibular Ligament; F—Calcaneofibular Ligament; G—Posterior Talocalcaneal Ligament; H—Posterior Talotibial Ligament; and I—Posterior Tibiofibular Ligament.

In the case of a *sprain fracture*, the pain will generally be above the joint instead of below it as with an ankle sprain (Morehouse and Rasch, 1963). It is common sense that the injured person must not use the ankle at all. Furthermore, immediate medical care is needed. The coach should elevate the injured ankle to help abate edema. Then, apply a compression bandage (but not too tight) followed by ice cold compresses.

Knee Sprains

Musculoskeletal Anatomy and Predisposing Factors. The primary movements at the knee joint are flexion and extension. However, medial and lateral rotation is possible when the knee is flexed. In that rotary movements accompanied by undue stress predispose the gymnast to knee injuries, a discussion of the related myology and ligamentous support is illustrated and clarified for greater appreciation of knee problems.

Landing in an unnatural position for the knee joint may result in a knee injury. Since the integrity of the knee is greatly dependent upon related musculature than ligamentous support, the conditioning program must develop these muscles and maintain their strength capability. The quadriceps femoris muscle, e.g., insures adequately anterior stabilization while the hamstring muscles, gastrocnemius, and the popliteus provide posterior stabilization of the knee joint (Logan and McKinney, 1970).

Strength per se, however, will not insure no injuries. Direct trauma (force) to the knee joint in a flexed position is generally all that is needed to injure the ligaments. Twisting tumbling skills and uncontrolled dismounts may produce forced abduction causing the medial (tibial) collateral ligament to rupture and/or medial meniscus injury (Morehouse and Rasch, 1963). Both the tibia (medial) and the fibula (lateral) collateral ligaments are more relaxed when the knee is flexed than when it is extended (straight). The flexed position with relaxed collaterals allow lateral and medial rotation which would otherwise not exist.

Additional stability is secured from the anterior and posterior cruciates (with their cross-configuration). All four ligaments are illustrated in Figure 11-4. Upon injuring the cruciates (singularly or both), there will be increased forward (anterior) and backward (posterior) movement at the knee joint (Rasch and Burke, 1967).

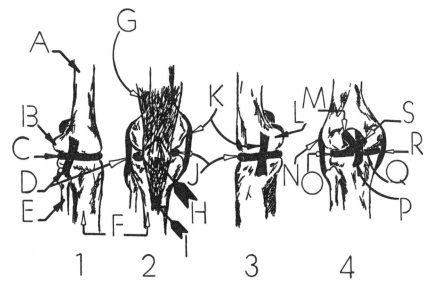

Figure 11-4: Illustration of the Ligaments and Cartilage Supporting the Knee Joint. (1) Lateral View, Right Leg: A—Femur; B—Lateral Condyle; C—Lateral Meniscus; D—Fibular Collateral Ligament; E—Fibula; and F—Tibia. (2) Anterior View, Right Leg: G—Tendon of Quadriceps Femoris; H—Patella; and I—Tibial Tuberosity. (3) Medial View, Right Leg: J—Medial Meniscus; K—Tibial Collateral Ligament; and L—Medial Condyle. (4) Posterior View, Left Leg: M—Anterior Cruciate Ligament; N—Fibular Collateral Ligament; O—Lateral Meniscus; P—Posterior Cruciate Ligament; Q—Medial Meniscus; R—Tibial Collateral Ligament; and S—Menisco-Femoral Ligament.

Treatment and Rehabilitative Procedures for Knee Sprains. When it is evident that a gymnast has injured his knee, investigate and determine the approximate area of pain and tenderness. If the medial meniscus is injured, the pain will be on the medial side of the knee joint. However, the extent of damage may or may not denote the severity of pain. Damage may occur without much distracting pain, although this is unusual. To avoid further internal complications, the coach must insist that a doctor examine the knee injury to determine the extent of damage. The coach can apply a cold compress while en route to the doctor to abate internal tissue bleeding.

Rehabilitation begins with surgical correction, rest, and mild to moderate use of progressive resistance exercises. Mild stress is needed to keep the muscles from wasting (atrophy).

Lumbar Sprains

Musculoskeletal Anatomy and Predisposing Factors. The vertebral column is divided into basically three curves (cervical, thoracic, and lumbar), but a sacral curve exists too (Figure 11-5a). These curves are normal and generally without pain or discomfort. Abnormal curves may denote some degree of potential complication. Lordosis (an exaggeration of the anterior convexity of the normal lumbar curve), e.g., increases the possibility of low-back problems (Figure 11-5b).

Muscular imbalances create the lordotic curve. The psoas major, e.g., originates from the anterior aspect of all five lumbar vertebrae and inserts on the lesser trochanter of the femur (Figure 11-6). Therefore, when one does straight-leg

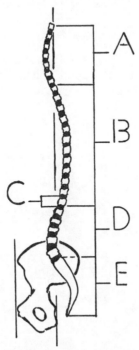

Figure 11-5a: Lateral View of Vertebral Column with Normal Curves. A—Cervical Curve; B—Thoracic Curve; C—Intervertebral Disks; D—Lumbar Curve; and E—Sacral Curve.

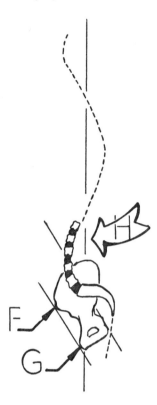

Figure 11-5b: Lateral View of Vertebral Column with LORDOSIS. F—Anterior Superior Iliac Spine; G—Pubic Crest; and H—Lordotic Curve.

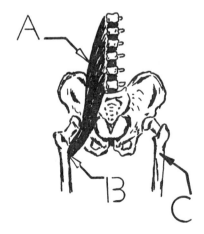

Figure 11-6: Anterior View of Psoas Major Muscle: Its Origin and Insertion. A—Psoas Major Muscle; B—Lesser Trochanter of the Femur; and C—Femur.

sit-ups, the weight of the upper body creates a forward movement (traction) of the lumbar spine at the psoas major muscle points of origin causing transient anterior convexity (lordosis). If a person habitually engages in such an exercise, the psoas muscle will shorten and resist stretch and elongation (Cailliet, 1962). When this occurs, the anterior superior iliac spine will be in front of the pubic crest (refer to Figure 11-5b).

Early Prevention and Treatment for a Lordotic Curve. The complications associated with lordosis may be counteracted by: (1) strengthening the rectus abdominis muscle to assist in maintaining a normal pubic crest position, which can be accomplished quite successfully by utilizing the bent-knee sit-up exercise; and (2) stretching and elongating the psoas and erecta spinae muscles to insure adequate hip flexion and extension. (Refer to Figure 11-7—a, b, c, and d—for further clarification.)

Figure 11-8 illustrates the ligaments that may be injured when undue stress and tension is placed on the lumbar region. For example, the author witnessed a gymnast injure his back upon dismounting from the rings. This dismount was a front flip. It was executed very poorly and required some compensation to land in the upright position. In so doing, the gymnast very vigorously opened from his tuck to realize that the unique extension caused the lumbar region to be hyperextended with subsequent pain, breathlessness, and discomfort. The next several days the gymnast was even more plagued by acute pain and stiffness. The coach advised the gymnast to see a doctor. Upon examination and X-ray, the doctor indicated that the pain and discomfort were due to ligamentous stretching.

The doctor felt, however, that the gymnast's lordosis (lumbo-sacral angle of 54 degrees) predisposed the athlete to the injury. Such an angle should be around 30 to 35 degrees. When the angle is more acute, the ligaments and related musculature must keep the lumbar vertebrae properly aligned.

Treatment and Rehabilitative Procedures for Lumbar Sprains. Treatment begins with discontinuing all stress to the lumbar region to induce healing and prevent further injury. The doctor's expert advice is a *must*. Physical manipulation and X-rays will indicate the extent of damage to the vertebrae proper. However, the extent of damage to the ligamentous structures is not so easily determined. Provided pain persists, the doctor will prescribe appropriate drugs and movement patterns to help alleviate predisposing factors. In addition, he will probably indicate not to sleep on the stomach if it causes low back pain. Rather, sleep on the side, back, or perhaps place a board under the mattress to keep it from sagging. Lastly, one could place a pillow under the legs, while on the back, to reduce tension on the iliopsoas muscles.

Shoulder and Shoulder Girdle Joint Sprains

Shoulder Musculoskeletal Anatomy and Predisposing Factors. The glenohumeral joint is susceptible to injury for several reasons: (1) the execution of a large number of gymnastic skills depends upon proper muscle and ligamentous stability; and (2) the

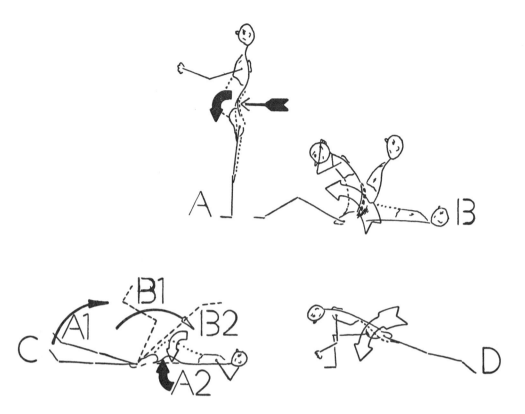

Figure 11-7: Relationship of Selected Muscles to Pelvic Alignment. (A) Relaxed rectus abdominis allows the pelvic girdle to tilt forward. Thus, the lumbar curved becomes more acute. (B) The bent-knee sit-up develops the rectus abdominis (prime mover) while the iliopsoas muscle acts as a helper. However, when one does straight-leg sit-ups, the iliopsoas muscle becomes the prime mover and may predispose one to an acute lumbar anterior convexity. (C)—A1 —Again, the iliopsoas is the prime mover with straight-leg raises. This exercise strengthens the hip flexors and not the rectus abdominis muscle. This exercise may also result in adaptive shortening of the erecta spinae muscles resulting in an increase lumbar curve as noted with illustration A2. An effective technique to stretch the low back, B1, is to bend the legs during the vertical lift followed by a straightening and lowering to the chest. This exercise will help to keep the lumbar spine flat (B2). (D) This exercise will stretch the hip flexors (iliopsoas) and probably aid in lessening anterior convexity of the lumbar region.

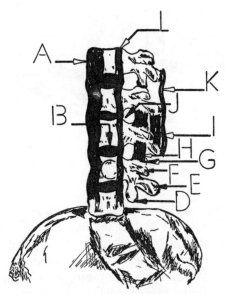

Figure 11-8: Ligaments of the Lumbar Vertebrae. A—Anterior Longitudinal Ligament; B—Intervertebrae Disc; C—Body; D—Inferior Articular Process; E—Spine; F—Transverse Process; G—Superior Articular Process; H—Ligamenta Flava; I—Interspinal Ligament; J—Intervertebral Foramen (containing nerve root); K—Supraspinal Ligament; and L—Posterior Longitudinal Ligament.

shoulder joint is not as stable as the hip joint (although both joints are referred to as ball-and-socket joints). The problem is that the humerus does not fit deep into the glenoid fossa; whereas, the femur does fit well within the acetabulum.

Both joints gain stability via their ligamentous binding and muscular support. The shoulder socket, e.g., is made deeper by the glenoidal labrum's (a ring of fibrocartilage acting like a meniscus) attachment to the margin of the glenoid fossa. This cavity receives the head of the humerus. The humerus is held within close proximity with the glenoid cavity by the attachment of several ligaments (refer to Figure 11-9).

The coracohumeral ligament extends from the coracoid process to the greater tubercle of the humerus. The three bands of the glenohumeral ligament arise basically from the superior and anterior borders of the glenoid cavity and over the head of the humerus. These two ligaments plus the encompassing capulse ligament provide the ligamentous support for shoulder joint stability. When a gymnast raises his arm (abduction) as in a handstand, the middle and inferior bands (glenohumeral ligament) become very tight while the superior band relaxes. The greater tension upon stretching serves to keep the head of the humerus in its proper place. When the arm is laterally rotated, as in a two-arm support on the parallel bars, all

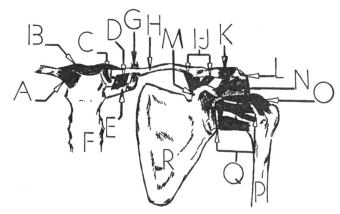

Figure 11-9: Anterior View of Sternoclavicular and Shoulder Joint Articulations and Ligamentous Support. A—Anterior Sternoclavicular Ligament; B—Interclavicular Ligament; C—Meniscus (articular disc); D—Costoclavicular Ligament; E—Costal Cartilage; F—Sternum; G—First Rib; H—Clavicle; I-J—Conoid and Trapezoid (coracoclavicular ligament); K—Acromioclavicular Ligament; L—Acromion; M—Coracoid Process; N—Coracoacromial Ligament; O—Coracohumeral Ligament; P—Humerus; Q—Glenohumeral (superior, middle, and inferior); and R—Scapula.

three bands are stretched to better secure the shoulder joint. Conversely, medial rotation relaxes the bands (Kapandji, 1970).

The anterior band of the coracohumeral ligament will stretch and create tension to maintain shoulder joint integrity when the arm is in extension. Therefore, when one swings on the parallel bars, the anterior band will pull on the lesser tuberosity of the humerus as the body swings forward leaving the arm in the extended position. The posterior band inserts on the greater tuberosity. During flexion, it will stretch to secure the head of the humerus, e.g., during the back swing. Thus, the ligaments do provide some stability. The shoulder joint is certainly more stable when both the ligaments and the muscles work together as is evident with knee joint stability.

The integrity of the shoulder joint is greatly dependent upon the rotator cuff muscles. Figure 11-10 illustrates three of the four rotary cuff muscles. They are the supraspinatus, infraspinatus, and teres minor muscles. Not shown is the subscapularis which arises from the subscapular fossa of the scapular and inserts on the humerus. All four muscles arise from the scapula and insert on the tubercules of the humerus. In effect, the four tendons of these muscles act as ligaments keeping the head of the humerus against the glenoid cavity.

The *acromioclavicular joint* is susceptible to injury when one lands on the top of

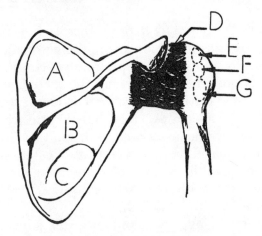

Figure 11-10: The Tendon Sites Which Form the Rotator Cuff (musculotendinous cuff) Muscles. A-E—Supraspinatus; B-F—Infraspinatus; C-G—Teres Minor; and D—Capsular Ligament.

the shoulder. This can happen when one fails to complete a back flip and lands on the shoulder proper. The injury may be to the ligaments (coracoclavicular) binding the clavicle to the scapula or the ligament (acromioclavicular) binding the clavicle to the acromion. Depending upon the severity of the injury, the acromioclavicular ligament may tear completely causing an acromioclavicular separation. Thus, the acromial end of the clavicle will be elevated. There will also be localized joint pain. Complications may be in the order of chipped or more involved acromion fractures.

The coracoclavicular ligament (refer to Figure 11-9) protects the acromion or scapula proper by transferring forces acquired from the side to the clavicle and eventually to the sternoclavicular joint (Kelley, 1971). This is the case since the lateral end of the clavicle joins the acromion by the acromioclavicular ligament and joins the coracoid process by the coracoclavicular ligaments (the conoid and the trapezoid ligaments). These three ligaments act together to help dissipate lateral forces to the acromion which would otherwise cause an acromioclavicular separation or shoulder sprain.

Treatment and Rehabilitative Procedures for Shoulder Sprains. A shoulder sprain is evident when one or several tendons of the rotator cuff muscles are stretched and irritated. Disrupting normal continuity of the tendons results in noticeable swelling and tenderness of the shoulder region. As with all tendon or ligamentous sprains, treatment consists of rest and the use of a sling (if necessary) to reduce unnecessary stress on the injured ligaments. Rehabilitation is a slow process depending upon the degree of injury, etc. Morehouse and Rasch (1963) indicate the use of: (1) mild heat on a regular basis; (2) analgesic compresses followed by gentle massage; (3) progressive strength building exercises; and (4) an adhesive support.

Treatment and Rehabilitative Procedures for Acromioclavicular Separations. An acromioclavicular separation is a serious injury involving the acromioclavicular ligament. An AC separation is actually an extension sprain in which the ligament has been partially or completely ruptured, thus allowing the scapula (acromion) to slide beneath the lateral end of the clavicle. The elevated clavicle appears as a lump at the top of the shoulder. With normal AC joint integrity destroyed, the use of the arm (as in lifting) is minimal and associated with mild to extreme pain. Upon recognizing the extent of damage, treatment consists of cold compresses to control tissue bleeding. Mild damage to the ligaments of and medially to the AC joint will heal with proper rest and care. With more severe injuries, surgical correction may be necessary to properly secure the AC joint.

As forces are transferred along the shoulder girdle joints, the *sternoclavicular joint* may also be injured (Figure 11-9). This joint comprises the medial end of the clavicle and the lateral side of the sternum. An intra-articular disc (cartilage) lies between the clavicle and the sternum to act as a shock buffer. The medial end of the clavicle can move in numerous directions depending upon the forces transmitted from the shoulder. This capacity to move up and down, forward and backward is certainly a desirable way to absorb force without injury.

To further prevent injury, the sternoclavicular ligaments (anterior and posterior) are designed to prevent lateral and upward displacement of the clavicle. The interclavicular ligament connects both clavicles to a common ligament which serves to prevent further lateral displacement of the clavicles. The costoclavicular ligament connects the clavicle to the first costal cartilage (first rib). It prevents upward and forward movement of the clavicle.

A *sternoclavicular sprain* involves the ligamentous support of the sternoclavicular joint. Since the ligaments are the primary means of support and maintenance of integrity, any injury to this joint should be handled basically in the same manner as with an AC sprain or separation.

Shoulder Dislocations

Musculoskeletal Anatomy and Predisposing Factors. A glenohumeral dislocation refers to a shoulder dislocation in which the articular surfaces of the head of the humerus and the glenoid cavity are no longer in proper anatomic contact. A fall that places undue force on an abducted, laterally rotated humerus may produce an anterior dislocation of the shoulder. The head of the humerus is displaced anteriorly as evident by an elevation beneath the coracoid process. The anterior dislocation is also called a subcoracoid dislocation due to the anterior-inferior relationship to the coracoid process (Figure 11-11).

Since the head of the humerus has dropped below its normal position, the support needed to keep the shoulder rounded is absent and thus the deltoid will appear flatter. O'Donoghue (1962) points out that the unique disarticulation of the joint will not allow the forearm to move across in front of the body. Conversely, with forceful medial rotation while the humerus is adducted, the head of the

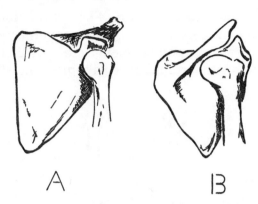

Figure 11-11: A—Subcoracoid (anterior) Dislocation; and B—Subspinous (posterior) Dislocation.

humerus will part posteriorly. Ryan (1962) states that posterior dislocations are not too common due to the strong tendinous attachment of the rotator cuff muscles. Posterior dislocations are evident by an increased fullness posteriorly.

Treatment and Rehabilitative Procedures for Shoulder Dislocations. When a dislocation is suspected, the injured arm must not be moved. It should be supported and immobilized. Symptoms are swelling, skin blanching, and coldness of the injured area. These symptoms will become more intense the longer the joint is disarticulated. Muckle (1971) states that unless the dislocation is very recurrent, it should not be reduced until the possibility of a fracture is ruled out. This approach is supported by Bronner and other medical authorities as well. They feel that irreparable damage may result when an untrained person attempts to reduce a dislocation. The best first aid procedure before medical aid is obtained is immobilization of the injured arm. To do otherwise may result in damage to nerves, arteries, ligaments, and related musculature. In essence, the coach's responsibility is one of preventing unnecessary damage to the shoulder and axilla region.

Rehabilitation of the shoulder begins after sufficient time has elapsed to permit the ligamentous and other structures about the joint to heal. The use of strength building exercises would appear to enhance the stability of the shoulder joint. It is important to avoid exercises which subject the injured joint to unneeded stress and strain. However, exercises which strengthen shoulder muscles are beneficial as they will compensate for the weaker structures. The superior aspect of the joint capsule and the supraspinatus, e.g., will prevent downward dislocation (MacConaill and Basmajian, 1969). Therefore, exercises to increase the strength of the rotator cuff muscles are not only beneficial, but mandatory.

Elbow Sprains and Dislocations

Musculoskeletal Anatomy and Predisposing Factors. It is said that the elbow joint is a complicated joint containing three individual articulations. The ulna and humerus articulation permits flexion and extension. The articulation of the radius and humerus permits flexion and extension too, but rotation is possible as well.

Joint stability is dependent upon ligaments and musculature. Refer to Figure 11-12 for the ligamentous support and articulations of the elbow joint.

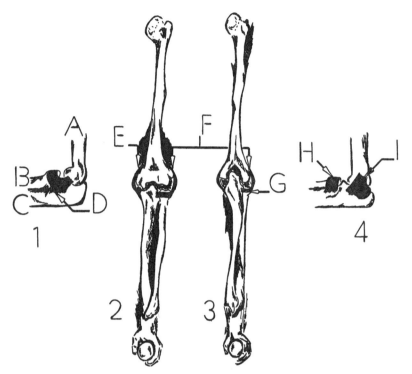

Figure 11-12: Ligamentous Support and Articulation of the Elbow Joint. A—Humerus; B—Radius; C—Ulna; D—Radial (lateral) Collateral Ligament; E—Ulnar (medial) Collateral Ligament; F—Radial (lateral) Collateral Ligament; G—Annular Ligament; H—Annular Ligament; and I—Ulnar (medial) Collateral Ligament. 1—Lateral View; 2—Anterior View (left arm); 3—Posterior View (right arm); and 4—Medial View.

The radio-ulna articulation is entirely dependent upon the annular ligament encircling the radial head. This ligament serves to keep the radius in its proper place against the radial fossa of the ulna.

The ulna collateral ligament (medial ligament) has three parts: (1) anterior; (2) intermediate; and (3) posterior. Upon elbow extension, the anterior band becomes stretched, securing the joint. Conversely, this band relaxes during flexion and the other bands tighten. This ligament helps to prevent abduction displacement (Kelly) and also strengthens the orbicular ligament (Kapandji). The lateral ligament stabilizes the elbow joint by restricting adduction displacement. It also strengthens the continuity of the annular ligament.

An *elbow sprain* is evident in cases where an uncontrolled or unsuspected force pushes the ulna away from the humerus, e.g., reaching back with an hyperextended arm to break a fall. Since the medial ligament restricts the articulation between the ulna and the humerus, it will be stretched when the forearm is hyperextended. Generally, however, the arm will immediately regain a flexed position with concomitant sensations of pain and tenderness around the ligamentous support of the joint.

All the ligaments are subject to tears, depending upon the intensity and direction of force applied at the joint. For example, a particular fall which forces excess adduction will injure the lateral ligament because it helps to restrict adduction displacement.

Treatment Procedures for Elbow Sprains. Tenderness on the surface will indicate possible underlying tears and injury. Cold compresses will help to control tissue bleeding and swelling. The gymnast should be instructed not to use the arm to allow adequate time for the ligaments to heal. As symptoms subside, the elbow should probably be strapped before intense participation. This is just a precautionary measure and can be stopped upon realizing full range of motion.

Treatment and Rehabilitative Procedures for Elbow Dislocations. An *elbow dislocation* requires a force that will rupture the stabilizing collateral ligaments. If these ligaments are not ruptured, the injury is a sprain and not a dislocation. However, the arm position is generally the same for both injuries, e.g., hyperextension.

The force applied in the hyperextended position lessens elbow joint stability with subsequent separation of the articulating surfaces. The coach should determine the extent of damage by palpation. If the inspection reveals deformity, swelling, and a loss of normal movement, an ice pack should be applied to the injured area to help control bleeding and tissue swelling. The arm must not be used to support the weight or objects, etc. In fact, it should be immobilized by placing the arm in a sling or by holding the injured arm near the body. Then the gymnast must be taken to a physician as quickly as possible. The results from treatment greatly depend upon the time from the injury and correction. The physician will reduce the dislocation. The coach must avoid any attempt to do so for fear of injury and complications to the nerves and arteries.

The gymnast must realize that adequate time is needed for proper rehabilitation. Full extension will not be possible at first nor should the arm be forcefully extended. Passive, gentle manipulation of the injured arm will benefit recovery. Upon being able to extend the arm without discomfort, the use of a progressive, conditioning program will strengthen and restore functional strength and a full range of movement. However, exercises which tend to overextend the elbow joint should be avoided.

Wrist and Hand Sprains-Dislocations

Musculoskeletal Anatomy and Predisposing Factors. The radius, ulna, and carpal bones form the wrist joint. The union is completed by ligamentous support. Figure 11-13 is a dorsal view of selected ligamentous support of the right hand. The ulnar collateral ligament connects the lower end (styloid process) of the ulnar to certain carpal bones in the proximal row. Likewise, the dorsal radiocarpal and radial collateral ligaments stabilize the articulation of the radius with other carpal bones of the first row. Although both the anterior and the posterior sides are abundantly supplied with ligaments, they do not impede movement or motion in the radiocarpal joint. Therefore, it is said that injury to this joint involves musculotendinous structures rather then ligaments per se.

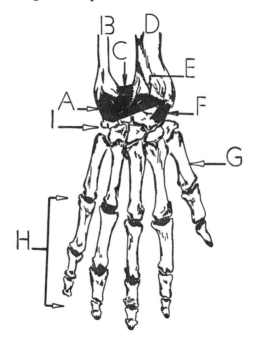

Figure 11-13:   Dorsal View of Selected Ligamentous Support of the
Right Wrist Joint. A—Ulnar Collateral Ligament;
B—Fibula; C—Dorsal Radioulnar Ligament;
D—Tibia; E—Dorsal Radiocarpal Ligament;
F—Radial Collateral Ligament; G—Metacarpal
Bones; H—Phalanges; and I—Carpal Bones.

Treatment and Rehabilitative Procedures for Wrist Sprains. A wrist sprain is not too different from a wrist strain when it comes to inspection and treatment of the injury. Any deformity of the wrist is usually followed by localized swelling of the injured area. However, general or extensive swelling may negate any attempt to palpate the injury. Tenderness in one specific area will help to determine the site of injury. An X-ray of the injury may be necessary to rule out possible fractures and dislocations of the carpal bones.

The duration of treatment depends upon the severity of the wrist sprain. Mild to moderate sprains can be treated as indicated with other sprains. Ice and elevation are helpful techniques to control the swelling and tissue bleeding. Later, heat may be useful in adjunct with passive exercises. Until tenderness and swelling subside, the wrist joint should be immobilized by adhesive strapping to protect it from extra strain and tension. Severe sprains may need more attention and immobilization to reduce any possibility of later complications.

Rehabilitation begins upon realizing the eventual recovery from the injury. Again, a strength building program may be beneficial. The longer one abstains from exercise, the weaker the joint becomes. Thus, it is essential that when exercises do not hinder but enhance joint stability, they should be done with some consistency and regularity.

A common lesion of the carpus is the *dislocation of the semilunar (lunate) bone*. This injury occurs when the hand must absorb excessive force upon falling. Figure 11-14 illustrates the relationship of lunate injury and dorsiflexion (hyperextension). Forceful hyperextension will dislocate the lunate bone with concomitant injury to the dorsal carpal ligament.

Figure 11-14: Hyperextension of the Left Hand with Dislocation of the Carpal Semilunar Bone.

The symptoms are mild to moderate swelling on the volar (palm side) surface. The presence of the lunate will produce pain and tenderness on the dorsum. If the lunate is not lodged under volar ligaments, motion will not be too restricted although the hand will probably be slightly flexed. Extension of the hand and fingers will produce intense pain due to medial nerve compression.

Treatment Procedures for Lunate Dislocations. Treatment entails immediate medical supervision. If detected early enough, the wrist joint and lunate can be manipulated (close reduction) so as to allow the lunate to slip back into its normal place. The success of this technique is dependent upon immediate closed reduction. If too much time elapses from the injury to time of correction, the place for the lunate bone will decrease in size and prevent any such movement from occurring. Thus, surgical intervention may be necessary.

Provided reduction is possible, both the hand and the wrist will be immobilized for some three weeks. Any force which attempts to dorsiflex the wrist must be avoided or at least kept to a minimum. During this time, adhesive strapping will add support and encourage recovery.

Thumb and Finger Dislocations

Musculoskeletal Anatomy and Predisposing Factors. A thumb or finger dislocation can occur when a force overcomes the normal stability of the respective joints. A posterior dislocation of the proximal phalanx of the thumb, a lateral dislocation of a finger at the articulation of the middle and proximal phalanges, a dorsal dislocation of the second phalanx, and compound dislocations of the phalanges are several examples of thumb and finger injuries that may be encountered when one uses the hands to absorb excessive forces to control and manipulate the body as in, e.g., gymnastics.

Treatment Procedures for Phalangeal Dislocations. Treatment depends upon the severity of the dislocation, the type, and the degree of complications such as chips, etc. It is still undecided whether it is best to reduce a dislocation in the gymnasium. If the displacement does not appear to be too involved and the palpation of the injured area reveals no abnormal developments, it may be possible to reduce and treat immediately. However, it is wise to remember that a complication of dislocations may be a small chip fracture.

An injured finger should be strapped to a good finger. Elevation is desirable to help reduce swelling. At the end of 1 to 3 weeks of strapping, the splint can be removed with subsequent passive to active exercises. The gymnast should avoid the exercises which may place undue strain on the recovery phase.

SPECIFIC FRACTURE TYPES

Fractures occur when a direct or indirect force disrupts normal bone continuity. The end result is moderate to extreme deformity and disability accompanied by various degrees of soft-tissue injury. The fracture itself may be one or several of six or seven types of fractures. The symptoms are: (1) shortening, due to the pull of the muscles; (2) swelling, due to tissue edema or tissue bleeding; (3) tenderness and pain, due to injury of sensory nerves; and (4) crepitation and restricted motion to mention a few.

Complications Resulting from Fractures

The complications of fractures may be the injury to muscles and tendons in the immediate area of the fracture. The muscles undergo considerable atrophy during immobilization of the injured limb. Occasionally, injuries to arteries and veins within the vicinity of the fracture will occur. An injury of this kind may lead to a false aneurysm or an extensive hematoma. Injury to motor and sensory nerves accompany fractures of the arm and elbow joint. Displacement of the fragmented bones may cut, stretch, or compress the nerves in the vicinity. Thus, a fractured humerus may lead to paralysis of specific muscles of the forearm or hand. This is the reason the doctor will administer a thorough neurological examination. That is, to determine if and which nerves are damaged based on paralysis of specific muscles. The symptoms of nerve damage are pain, tingling, and numbness. Moreover, a femur or humeral fracture may result in direct or indirect injury to the knee joint and elbow joint respectively (Key and Conwell, 1951).

Treatment Procedures for Specific Fractures

First aid in fractures is necessary for two reasons: (1) to determine the extent of damage as best possible (e.g., is the injury trivial or does it need immediate emergency treatment?); and (2) to administer emergency treatment to prevent further complications.

Emergency treatment entails the immobilization of the injured part. The athlete should be scrutinized for possible shock. Do not allow him to get cold nor to be moved when such movement may predispose him to pain and injury. Instead, use a sling, or splint the fracture to restrict movement above and below the injury (fracture).

Fractures of the Spine. When suspected fractures of the spine exist, the injured person *must not* be flexed. Flexion of the spine can result in extensive damage to the spinal cord. Severing the cord may result in paralysis depending upon the level (cervical, thoracic, or lumbar) of injury. Symptoms are spinal pain, restricted or inability to move, tingling and numbness sensations followed by loss of both with subsequent recovery later after swelling subsides. The spine should be maintained in a hyperextended position if transportation and movement is necessary.

Fractures of the Clavicle. This is a common athletic injury and is usually the result of falling on an outstretched hand. The outstretched arm and hand absorb the force, reducing the impact of the fall. However, sometimes too much force can be transmitted to the clavicle, which often results in a complete fracture. The proximal part (that nearest the sternum) will tend to be lifted by the action of the sternocleidomastoid muscle. The distal portion will be pulled downward and to the side as a result of the deltoid and pectoralis major muscles (Brantigan, 1963).

Emergency care entails the stabilization of the shoulder region by the use of a band holding the elbow in its proper place with the shoulder, a band to keep the arm against the body, and a sling to support the forearm and arm. This reduces both the downward displacement of the distal fragment of the clavicle and the extraneous motion.

Supracondylar Fractures. A forceful fall on the hand while the elbow is bent will produce a supracondylar fracture. This is a fracture of the humerus just above the condyles. It is a very serious fracture in that traumatic and permanent injury to arteries and nerves is inevitable if treatment is not obtained as quickly as possible. The arm will be deformed, disabled, painful, and swollen. Immobilize the injured arm and rush the athlete to a doctor for reduction.

Colles' Fractures. A similar force as described earlier may also produce a Colles' fracture, which is a fracture of the radius in close vicinity of the carpal bones. The same emergency care procedures previously denoted also apply in this case. Immobilize the forearm and hand, and promptly seek medical correction.

Pott's Fractures. The Colle's fracture is very similar to the fracture about the ankle (Pott's fracture). In this case, either or both malleoli of the tibia and/or fibula will fracture. Generally, the force for this fracture is transmitted via the strong ankle-joint ligaments discussed earlier. Which malleolus is fractured depends upon the direction and continuation of the force. A strong eversion, e.g., is counteracted by the deltoid ligament of the ankle joint. If the force overcomes the strength of the ligament, it will tear or rupture. But, if the ligament does not tear, the force is transmitted to the tibial malleolus resulting in a fracture. Conversely, as a direct inversion force supersedes the inherent stability of the fibula, it will fracture. If the same force is continued throughout the ankle joint, it may result in damage or fracture of the tibia as well (Brantigan).

Scaphoid Fractures. Muckle states that the most critical injury of the wrist is the scaphoid fracture. The mechanism of injury involves a force while the hand is dorsiflexed. There is localized tenderness, mild swelling, etc., but the fracture is elusive. In fact, some two or three weeks may pass before an X-ray depicts the fracture(s). The critical aspect of this injury entails the danger of blood flow interference, and thus avascular necrosis is a potential outcome without adequate medical guidance and correction.

Fractures of the Skull. Skull fractures are not common in gymnastics, but the possibility is built into the complexity of many skills. The fracture appears to be of little interest to the doctor. He is more interested in determining if damage has occurred to the brain and its blood vessels. The displacement of the fracture can certainly produce brain damage as well as predisposing the person to infection (meningitis) and extensive arterial bleeding.

The coach *must* consider head injuries as very dangerous. He should take the injured athlete to the doctor for medical examination, X-rays, etc. Do not waste time. Depending upon the location of the injury, bleeding from the middle meningeal artery can result in an accumulation of blood between the bone and the dura (extradural haematoma). The person may or may not be knocked unconscious, but eventually the pressure of the haematoma will disrupt normal brain function resulting in brain damage and possibly paralysis. If the injury causes arterial and venous rupturing between the arachoid and dura (subdural haematoma), the symptoms may not appear until some time later. The presence of the blood clot will also disrupt normal brain activity, resulting in post-traumatic epilepsy and/or intense headaches. Treatment for extradural and subdural haematomas is surgical removal of the blood clot. The pressure on the brain is relieved, and thus recovery is good.

Fortunately, head injuries in gymnastics are very few. Rather, a fall on the head may result in unconsciousness or just a shaken-up feeling referred to as a *concussion*. A *contusion* is a more serious concussion. The brain is damaged with loss of certain functions dependent upon the dead brain cells (Bickerstaff, 1965).

When one falls on the head, he may not lose consciousness. A loss of consciousness denotes possible damage to the reticular formation. A function of the reticular formation is to keep the brain aroused. Without the neural impulses to do so, the brain is unaroused (loss of consciousness).

What should the coach do for the unconscious athlete? Since there are different levels of consciousness (drowsiness, stupor, and coma), the coach should probably try and determine the level of consciousness. If the unconscious person is not breathing, administer mouth to mouth respiration. Examine the pupils. Extensive internal arterial damage results in pressure and damage to the third cranial nerve, causing the pupils to dilate. If one pupil is dilated, get the person to the doctor at *once*. At any rate, the injured person must be taken to the doctor for medical examination, X-rays, etc. Before and during the trip, do not give liquids if the person is unconscious. An attempt to do so may cause death due to the fluid entering the lungs. Also, do not neglect the possibility of other injuries, e.g., spinal fractures (Muckle).

BLISTERS AND CALLUSES

Any activity (work, pleasure, or otherwise) that requires constant contact for accomplishment will ultimately produce friction. The struggle to keep one's grip while the hands get hotter and become more irritated creates the inevitable frustrations and discomforts inherent with blisters and calluses.

Blisters may disable the gymnast if acute and/or not treated properly. Therefore, it is necessary to know how to treat blisters both preventively and therapeutically. Most coaches have witnessed the two commonly practiced techniques of handling blisters. They are:

1. Aspirate the blister leaving the distended external flap intact.

2. Aspirate the blister, and then remove the distended skin leaving the blister exposed.

Both techniques can be successful and troublesome, the second one being particularly painful when a determined gymnast continues his workout on the exposed area. In fact, this procedure may result in an infection as well.

Treatment begins with keeping the palms from becoming overcalloused. Charteris (1969) states that large calluses may actually produce blisters under the callus. Moreover, large calluses distract from normal healing due to high, uneven callus remains. Do not allow the calluses to get too large. Watch out for the hot spot irritations that eventually become blisters. Thus, *prevent* rather than treat blisters.

Keep the callosity from becoming acute by using lanolin ointment on the keratinized area or simply cut the excessive calluses from the palmar area. Do not play around. These injuries must be adequately treated if not prevented, or otherwise performance (mentally and physically) will suffer.

REFERENCES

Bicherstaff, Edwin R. *Neurology for Nurses.* London: The English Universities Press LTD, 1965.

Brantigan, Otto C. *Clinical Anatomy.* New York: McGraw-Hill Book Company, Inc., 1963.

Brunner, Lillian S., Charles P. Emerson, Jr., L. Kraeer Ferguson, and Doris S. Suddarth. *Textbook of Medical-Surgical Nursing.* Philadelphia: J. B. Lippincott Company, 1970.

Caillient, Rene. *Foot and Ankle Pain.* Philadelphia: F. A. Davis Company, 1968.

Caillient, Rene. *Low Back Pain Syndrome.* Philadelphia: F. A. Davis Company, 1962.

Caillient, Rene. *Neck and Arm Pain.* Philadelphia: F. A. Davis Company, 1964.

Charteris, Jack. *This Is Gymnastics.* Champaign, Illinois: Stipes Publishing Co., 1969.

Crouch, James E. *Functional Human Anatomy.* Philadelphia: Lea and Febiger, 1965.

Dayton, O. William. *Athletic Training and Conditioning.* New York: The Ronald Press Company, 1965.

Frost, H. M. *An Introduction to Biomechanics.* Springfield, Illinois: Charles C. Thomas, 1967.

Gray, Henry. *Anatomy of the Human Body.* Charles M. Goss (Ed.), 28th ed., Philadelphia: Lea and Febiger, 1966.

Henderson, John. *Emergency Medical Guide.* New York: McGraw-Hill Book Company, 1969.

Hirata, Jr., Isao. *The Doctor and the Athlete.* Philadelphia: J. B. Lippincott Company, 1968.

Kapandiji, I. A. *The Physiology of the Joints.* Teviot Place, Edinburgh: E. and S. Livingstone, 1970.

Key, John Albert, and H. Earle Conwell. *The Management of Fractures, Dislocations, and Sprains.* St. Louis: The C. V. Mosby Company, 1951.

Logan, Gene A. *Adaptations of Muscular Activity.* Belmont, California: Wadsworth Publishing Company, Inc., 1964.

Logan, Gene A., and Wayne C. McKinney. *Kinesiology.* Dubuque, Iowa: Wm. C. Brown Company Publishers, 1970.

MacConaill, M. A., and J. V. Basmajian. *Muscles and Movements: A Basis for Human Kinesiology.* Baltimore, Maryland: The Williams and Wilkins Company, 1969.

Mathews, Donald K., Ralph W. Stacy, and George N. Hoover. *Physiology of Muscular Activity and Exercise.* New York: The Ronald Press Company, 1964.

Morehouse, Laurence E., and Philip J. Rasch. *Sports Medicine for Trainers.* Philadelphia: W. B. Saunders Company, 1963.

Muckel, David S. *Sports Injuries.* England: Oriel Press, 1971.

O'Donoghue, Don H. *Treatment of Injuries to Athletes*. Philadelphia: W. B. Saunders Company, 1962.

O'Shea, John Patrick. *Scientific Principles and Methods of Strength Fitness*. Reading, Massachusetts: Addison-Wesley Publishing Company, 1969.

Rasch, Philip J., and Roger K. Burke. *Kinesiology and Applied Anatomy*. Philadelphia: Lea and Febiger, 1971.

Ryan, Allan J. *Medical Care of the Athlete*. New York: The McGraw-Hill Book Company, Inc., 1962.

Ryan, Allan J. "The Physician and Exercise Physiology," Ch. 11 in *Exercise Physiology*, Harold B. Falls (Ed.). New York: Academic Press, 1968.

Wickstrom, Ralph L. "More Careful Treatment for Hand Injuries," *Athletic Journal*. Vol. 53, No. 5, (January, 1973), pp. 42, 44, 76.

PART IV

The Biomechanics of Gymnastics

A biomechanical approach to gymnastic coaching is urgently needed for a sound foundation from which meaningful and relevant teaching and coaching techniques may emerge.

Chapter 12 examines the basic principles of motion, equilibrium, and force relative to coaching gymnastics. Chapter 13 deals with an application of biomechanical laws and principles to specific gymnastic skills as they relate to men's Olympic events (floor exercise, parallel bars, horizontal bar, still rings, side horse, and vaulting).

The importance of studying biomechanical applications to gymnastics lies in the additional understanding and insight into efficient and mechanically correct human motion. Hence, Part IV will certainly aid the gymnastic coach in developing into an effective leader and respected coach.

12

The Place for Biomechanics in Coaching Gymnastics

Most coaches are concerned with controlling and utilizing forces that may ultimately enhance the execution of sport skills. Gymnastic coaches are generally more aware of forces and outcomes than a track coach or a basketball coach. Moreover, gymnasts and their coaches often converse with concern for teaching and/or learning techniques. Improvement in physical performance occurs more rapidly upon realizing the appropriateness of one technique over another technique. Logically then, the gymnastic coach should have a sound knowledge of biomechanics since it is a science concerned with forces and effects (Hay, 1973).

This chapter deals with a basic interpretation of the science of biomechanics (motion, equilibrium, and force) as it may be expressed through the sport of gymnastics. It is hoped that the information contained in this chapter with its immediate application to gymnastics will perpetuate the use of biomechanical principles to increase coaching effectiveness.

NEWTONIAN LAWS OF MOTION

Gymnastics is a very dynamic sport. It requires quick and precise changes in body and/or limb position, resulting in motion. Such motion is generally direction specific and controlled by a desired speed. Dynamic gymnastics is possible via internal and external forces (muscle contractions and gravity) sufficient to disrupt or overcome the body's inertia. A discussion of the three basic laws of motion as stated by Sir Isaac Newton will help clarify their application to sport skills, particularly gymnastics.

Law of Inertia

Newton's first law states that a body remains in a state of rest or uniform motion in a straight line unless overpowered by a force to overcome its inertia. Basically this law explains how a gymnast may remain in a handstand position, convert the static position into a dynamic swing, accelerate the swing, alter its direction, and bring the swing to a stop. That is, via both internal and external forces.

An example of these forces and subsequent movements is clearly visualized by an application to a gymnastic skill referred to as "handstand-stutz-handstand." The main points of interest are:

1. The beginning handstand position is one of static equilibrium. That is, the sum total of all forces acting on the gymnast to disrupt the handstand position is zero. Again, based on the Law of Inertia, the downward swing will not commence unless a force via muscle contraction is great enough to overcome inertia (the tendency to resist a change of motion or a state of rest).

2. Overcoming inertia of the downward swing (from the inverted to a support vertical position) is influenced and shaped by the intensity and magnitude of the internal forces more than the external force. While both forces and body position (piked or extended) add to the total effect, the speed of the down swing varies with the applied force or forces which may either retard or accelerate the descent.

3. The influence of gravity on the upward phase of the swing is counteracted by reducing the radius of rotation by assuming a more piked body position (resulting in an increased angular velocity). In addition, a greater muscular involvement (internal force) is needed: (1) to cope with the inertia inherent in motion via a straight line and in reference to the twisting phase of the up swing; and (2) to provide the ideal height (via linear and angular motion) upon finishing the twist and maintaining the handstand position. A continuation of force is needed to maintain static balance in that the gymnast's inertia (and momentum) makes it difficult to stop.

Not clearly defined in the above example relative to the law of inertia are several basic principles of sound coaching and performance (Jensen and Schultz, 1970). They are:

1. Performance or motion is either linear (translatory), angular (rotary), or a combination of both. Both linear (in some cases, curvilinear translation) and angular motions are the basic substance of many gymnastic skills. That is, voluntary forces result in movement (performance) via one or both types of motion, e.g., during the approach and execution of a front flip and tumbling skills such as

cartwheels (two-arm and one-arm), headsprings, and handsprings. A successful execution of these skills depends upon the proper integration of both types of motion. For example, an approach (linear motion) too fast to efficiently convert into a vertical lift and finally into rotary motion is a poor overall execution technique. To enhance the rotary motion in the front flip, e.g., the translatory motion must be of ideal velocity (not too fast or too slow). Conversely, if the gymnast fails to tuck properly, rotary motion will then distract from the ideal translatory motion. The solution is an efficient combination of both motions.

2. Not only is timing a crucial factor with sequential development of subsequent skills, but the continuity of each motion is important too. For example, the gymnast utilizes less energy performing a back hip circle on the high bar if he bends at the waist and pushes back and up prior to a complete encirclement of the bar. By increasing the descent distance and consequently linear motion, the resistance to the back hip circle motion is reduced. However, should the performer stop his linear motion (as some beginners will do) by coming to a complete stop before he attempts the hip circle, he will reduce his chances of success. That is, the loss of the first motion (curvilinear) fails to lessen the resistance (the difficulty experienced while trying to encircle the bar).

3. Most coaches realize the importance of transferring momentum from one part of the body to the total body, e.g., during a front flip. But some coaches often overlook the fact that an effective transfer is dependent upon whether the gymnast is in contact with the mat when the transfer of momentum is most urgently needed. Again, a gymnast attempting a peach basket to handstand on the parallel bars is as successful as his ability to maintain his grip to a point that complements the transfer of momentum from the piked position to the more extended body position. The vigorous lift (hip extension) of the legs transfers momentum from the legs to the body in a way that tends to aid its vertical progress.

Law of Acceleration

A change in velocity (acceleration) of a body is proportional to the force and in the same direction of the force. Newton's second law of motion is clearly visualized with the handstand-stutz-handstand example discussed earlier in reference to Newton's first law of motion. To continue the example, it is well recognized that the velocity of the swing must increase to continue the desired upward lift accommodating the twist phase. In this case, an increased internal force results in a proportional increase in velocity to overcome both linear and rotary resistances. A gymnast can increase acceleration by applying a greater force against the parallel bars.

Several basic principles of sound coaching and performance relative to the law of acceleration (Jensen and Schultz, 1970) and the movements of a pendulum (Wells, 1971) are:

1. A sequential application of all forces (producing a particular type of motion) is necessary for optimal execution of sport skills. Furthermore, unnecessary

forces should be controlled and reduced so as to negate their interference with maximum utilization of the more appropriate forces.

2. A swinging body (a pendulum) may increase its angular velocity by lengthening the radius of rotation on the down swing and shortening it on the beginning of the up swing (at the bottom of the arc and upwards). The manipulation of the body position reduces the resistance against both linear and angular motions.

3. The twisting phase of the stutz occurs primarily as a result of transfer of momentum. That is, a gradual or fast turning of a specific part of the body while supported facilitates the twisting action. In this case, the head and leg segments initially elicit the twisting movement. Upon release of the right hand (while the left hand remains as the support arm) and its quick movement across the body, the speed of the twist (rotation) is increased.

4. Upon realizing the end of the up swing (remember that the twist commences during the up swing and is generally completed at the peak of the up swing), the velocity is zero until the force of gravity produces the downward component felt during the regrasp phase. Friction between the hands and the bars aids the gymnast in developing and controlling the internal force (muscle contractions) and external forces (gravity and centrifugal force). Thus, the gymnast should use magnesium chalk to enhance his grip on the parallel bars or any other apparatus for that matter.

Law of Equal and Opposite Forces

Newton's third law of motion states that every force is accompanied by an equal and opposite force. Again, with reference to the earlier example, the weight of the gymnast and the force exerted downward via the swing is also matched by a counterforce. This force of the parallel bars complements the internal forces directing the path of the performer. Thus, the parallel bars push back with an equal and opposite force. In the case where the downward force exceeds the capacity of the bars to store and return the force to the performer, the bars will break.

Several basic principles of sound coaching and performance relative to the law of equal and opposite forces (Jensen and Schultz, 1970; and Rasch and Burke, 1971) are:

1. Regardless of whether one's grip slips or remains firm, the force applied results in an opposite force of the same magnitude. However, the counterforce may or may not be desirable and certainly not possible once the hands leave the bars. If a front flip requires a certain force for optimal performance, then a force less than the required results in a performance of less than desirable quality. Moreover, a poorly directed downward force (poor projection angle for a front flip) tends to result in a less than desired counterforce. In view of this, the counterforce is more effectively utilized as the downward force is more vertical to the tumbling mat.

2. To effectively use the properly integrated forces during the extension

phase of the peach basket to handstand, the grip must be securely maintained to use the stored force in the bars. That is, hip extension produces a force via the bars to the arms and trunk only if the grip is secured. Otherwise, the force generated by the hip extension action dissipates without an opportunity for an efficient expression.

This process whereby momentum is redistributed within the body is, in this case, greatly dependent upon a sound and effective use and release of the bars. If the flexor muscles of the forearms are too weak to maintain the proper grip, the performer will receive less propulsion for the amount of force applied. Thus, as the feet and legs begin to slow down (during the extension phase of the peach basket), the rest of the body fails to receive the expectant increase in angular momentum.

EQUILIBRIUM

Being able to control equilibrium, whether stationary or moving, is probably the deciding factor between the average and the excellent gymnast. An excellent gymnast appears to balance himself more easily and with less strain than the average athlete. The experienced and trained athlete is more efficient at adjusting the various forces that often interact to disrupt balance. Fortunately, an understanding and application of the principles of equilibrium will increase balance and stability (Broer, 1973; and Jensen and Schultz, 1970). They are:

1. With reference to a gymnast performing a handstand on the floor, in the rings, or on the parallel bars, he will remain in balance until the center of gravity passes outside the base. At this time, movement will occur in the direction of displacement of the line of gravity. Thus, to secure the handstand position, the gymnast should keep his center of gravity (weight) over the center of the base. The closer the center of his weight is over the base, the more stable he becomes.

2. It is recognized that the handstand position is harder to perform in the rings than on the parallel bars. During the intial learning attempts, a gymnast should not extend in the shoulder region as he is commonly taught and performs on the bars. Rather, he should assume a more relaxed shoulder position to increase his chances of maintaining static balance. Why? The relaxed shoulder position lowers the center of gravity, increasing stability. However, the beginner should not have an excessive arch in the lumbar region. The head should not be too high, but in more of a relaxed position.

3. Moreover, the base of support may be increased by placing the forearms against the straps. This also increases friction between the body and its base. This is often used by the beginner while attempting handstands in the rings. The technique does enhance learning because it increases stability. That is, the center of gravity can move more without passing over the base. This approach to increasing stability is often utilized when one forms a triangle prior to a headstand. The beginner usually places the head between the hands, which reduces the area of the base of support. Consequently, the beginner fails to attain a stable position until he

learns the necessity for making a triangle with his head and hands. The principle of increasing the size of the base is more critically realized when one attempts a skill with a smaller than usual base. A one-arm handstand, e.g., often results in great difficulty due to the very small base.

4. Stability is increased during forward or backward angular or rotary motion. Hence, a swing to a handstand followed immediately by a pirouette is generally easier than when one performs the same skill, yet from a stationary position. The initial learning period would obviously call for the stable position and not the dynamic one.

5. Finally, the ability to maintain balance in stationary and dynamic positions is highly dependent upon the ability of the athlete to interpret and effectively use kinesthetic and visual feedback. If a gymnast, e.g., closes his eyes while performing a handstand in the rings, he will probably fall immediately. Whereas, with the eyes open, he will probably maintain balance by correcting small movements which would otherwise result in displacement of the center of gravity outside the base of support. Gymnasts often bend the legs or arms to prevent falling from the handstand position. This technique lowers the center of gravity and makes the stabilizing process a little easier.

FORCE

A force is necessary for motion. Muscle contractions produce forces that may be manipulated to create desired movements—generally speaking, that of overcoming inertia and directing the body in a way that the desired results will be realized. A basic overview of two principles of production and magnitude of force are presented for the coach's consideration and application to gymnastics. First, a gymnast (upon beginning a floor exercise sequence) will remain at rest until a force is sufficient in magnitude to overcome the resistance to motion (inertia). Secondly, upon realizing that the first sequence involves a combination of tumbling skills, a gymnast should take 3-5 running steps instead of 1-2 steps for the most effective force. Thus, through a greater distance and time to accelerate and increase momentum, the skills requiring force are more easily accomplished.

In addition, a gymnast may express via the performance some difficulty with the sequence. He may lose control and fall. He may complete, e.g., 2 skills of a 5 skill sequence. Regardless of the problem (provided other factors are adequate such as strength, endurance, coordination, etc.) with one or several skills in the sequence, it usually stems from an inappropriate application of body mechanics. This is especially the case with force. The following principles of force are applied to the front flip for further clarification (Broer, 1973):

1. Assuming the first skill of the sequence is a front flip, the sum of the forces acquired from the run should be utilized in the same direction. To initiate a front flip in any direction other than in the line of the run will retard angular motion.

2. The faster the gymnast contracts the appropriate muscles to perform the front flip, the more force is produced and applied to enhance motion in the desired direction.

3. The force at takeoff will be greater if the gymnast's "foot-action" is one of heel-toe rather than a flat-footed lift. In this case, the longer a force is applied to the floor, the greater the force and velocity will be developed.

4. If a gymnast finalizes the vertical lift with a full extension of the legs (as opposed to a bent-knee position), the greater is the force that can be exerted. A muscle can exert more force when it is fully stretched.

5. The forces producing angular motion rise with the upper trunk, especially the arms and head. These forces are more effective if initiated when (or just as) the feet leave the mat. The gymnast will rotate when a force is applied while one segment of the body is fixed, e.g., during a giant swing on the high bar or a shoot to the handstand position on the rings.

6. Again, the higher (farther) the arms (as they may elicit the necessary rotary force) from the center of gravity, the less force required to produce rotation. This is clearly visualized when one attempts a front flip with no arm action. The attempt, in this case, requires a considerable muscular involvement to create the necessary forces for an adequate and safe rotation.

7. Upon completing the flip, the gymnast must not dissipate the force upon impact. Rather, the summation of forces (horizontal and vertical) must be efficiently transferred to the next skill in the sequence. Naturally, some of the force will be absorbed upon impact due to the flexed leg and hip position. However, the center of gravity must continue its flight forward outside the base of support. The continuation of the forces is realized in the handspring, the next skill. Thus, the execution of the handspring should be easier.

REFERENCES

Boone, Tommy. "Peach Basket to Handstand," *Athletic Journal*. Vol. 51, No. 3, (November, 1970), pp. 9, 52-54.

Broer, Marion R. *Efficiency of Human Movement*. Philadelphia: W. B. Saunders Company, 1973.

Hay, James G. *The Biomechanics of Sports Techniques*. Englewood Cliffs, N. J.: Prentice-Hall, Inc., 1973.

Jensen, Clayne R., and Gordon W. Schultz. *Applied Kinesiology*. New York: McGraw Hill Book Company, 1970.

Rasch, Philip J., and Roger K. Burke. *Kinesiology and Applied Anatomy*. Philadelphia: Lea and Febiger, 1971.

Wells, Katherine F. *Kinesiology*. Philadelphia: W. B. Saunders Company, 1971.

13

Application of Mechanical Laws and Principles to Gymnastics

Men's gymnastics is actually six distinct events placed under one title, *gymnastics*. It is generally expected that the participants perform in all six events, particularly if Olympic interests are prevalent.

This chapter deals with a comprehensive biomechanical discussion of specific skills as they relate to the men's Olympic events (floor exercise, parallel bars, horizontal bar, still rings, side horse, and vaulting). This discussion of specific skills illustrates one method of acquiring a greater understanding of skills per se as they relate to the difficult task of coaching. In this regard, it is hoped that the use of biomechanics as a coaching aid will come to permeate the analysis of gymnastic skills.

FLOOR EXERCISE

Handstand

An excellent gymnast can perform a handstand (inverted balance) on the floor, the bars, or on the rings. The principles of stability are the same regardless of the support. However, as a beginner gymnast progresses from the floor, to the bars, to the rings, he will experience increased difficulty dominating the skill.

The handstand is usually learned on the floor for two reasons: (1) the principles of balance are more easily applied without necessary compensations; and (2) the gymnast seldom experiences injury due to the safety mats and the lack of sufficient height to warrant potential or serious injury.

Floor. The general teaching technique dictates that the gymnast should place his hands on the mat. They should be about shoulder width apart. The fingers should be spread. The arms should be straight and laterally rotated (aids in locking the elbow joint). Thus, the gymnast is assured of a large base and a strong support to keep the center of gravity stable. As the skill gets easier, he may reach for the floor from a vertical or standing position. The arm movement aids in acquiring the necessary angular momentum to invert the body. However, this technique should not be used by the beginner. It will prolong the learning process. For example, an overly vigorous downward motion of the arms and/or an upward lift of the rear leg predisposes the performer to an uncontrolled rotary movement. Again, if the hands are placed too far from the body, the body may fail to gain the necessary angular momentum to attain the height prerequisite for an inverted balance. Hence, it is better to begin with the hands in contact with the floor. The forceful lift of the rear leg creates angular momentum which is imparted to the body, resulting in rotary movement. The body begins to take on a handstand appearance. At this time, the remaining leg vigorously extends, aiding in vertical lift and angular momentum (Law of Action-Reaction). Judging the intensity of the push from the floor is a troublesome task for the beginner. Too much or too little muscular action reduces the chances of securing the inverted position.

The inverted position is maintained by several rather common procedures, although gymnasts are generally unaware of the mechanics employed. They are:

1. A more forceful pressing of the fingers against the floor to oppose falling forward.

2. A slight to more acute hyperextension of the neck aids in opposing too much angular momentum.

3. The bending of the legs and arms separately or together tends to lower the center of gravity, increasing stability. Too much or too little angular momentum is brought under control by using this technique.

4. An arched handstand often compansates for a lack of adequate control of the center of gravity by moving it closer to the base.

5. Finally, the movement of the base of support (one hand at a time) may be necessary to keep the center of gravity within the base.

With severe loss of balance, the gymnast may employ one or all of these procedures to maintain stability. Obviously, the application of these procedures is not technically correct, but often physically rewarding in terms of safety.

Scales are performed with similar mechanics as used in handstands. A basic difficulty experienced when one attempts a scale (side, front, etc.) is the ability to maintain balance. Naturally, this is the case since the center of gravity must fall over the midpoint of a very small base. In addition, the lifting of a leg or arm (arms) often results in raising the center of gravity. Hence, instead of the center of gravity moving nearer to the base, and a base increasing in area over which the center of gravity may center itself, the direct opposite actually occurs. Provided the gymnast has good flexibility and at least an average feeling for integrating and utilizing both internal and external forces, the previously mentioned mechanical changes will be neutralized.

Parallel Bars. Handstands on the parallel bars require basically the same mechanical considerations as just discussed. At first, a gymnast will develop too little angular momentum, thus failing to attain the necessary height. However, when too much angular momentum is the case, the gymnast will pass through the handstand position. Again, he may compensate by walking in the handstand position to keep the base underneath the center of gravity.

A very safe and reliable method of learning the handstand on the P - bars is to avoid swinging to a handstand intentionally. Rather, one should progressively increase the forward and backward motion until the backward-vertical lift assumes the inverted position. In this way, the gymnast concentrates on the swing first and the handstand second. Otherwise, by thinking about the handstand, one often fails to control the swing. This creates the two conditions described earlier.

Once one acquires an adequate kinesthetic awareness of the body in the inverted position, the handstand is often said to be easier than when performed on the floor. And, to some extent, such an interpretation is correct since the grip is more powerful while grasping the bars as opposed to the extended wrist-position on the floor. The primary movements (forward-backward) disrupting balance can be more effectively counteracted to sustain stability.

Rings. A handstand on the rings is the most difficult of the three. The main problem is that the base of support (the rings and ropes) moves; whereas, the parallel bars and the floor do not move. So, when a gymnast exerts a force through the ropes, the reaction may be realized in a direction nonconducive for adequate vertical progress. Therefore, the energy spent to keep the base of support underneath the center of gravity is in addition to the energy expended to perform the handstand. Often, this is why gymnasts assume some arch in the back and allow the shoulder position to be less extended. That is, to lower the center of gravity and save on energy.

Hay (1973) states that a straight handstand requires less effort (energy) than an arched handstand. Apparently this conclusion was based on the interaction of two or more blocks, the center of gravity of each block, and the positioning of all blocks so as to imitate the two types of handstands. Upon examining the principles of an efficient inverted balance position, one can clearly see why the arched handstand position would seem to require more energy. The arched position, e.g., results in the forward displacement of the legs. When a segment of the body is out of line with the segment supporting it, gravity pulls it downward. In this case, gravity pulls the legs downward. The gymnast must exert energy to keep the legs straight (from falling). Whereas, if the legs were above the part (hips) supporting them, the handstand would appear to be more stable and require less energy since the center of gravity of both segments would fall on the same line (Broer, 1973).

However, there are other factors to consider that may utilize energy. If the gymnast extends the shoulders in addition to the so-called energy-saving straight handstand, the center of gravity is raised. More energy is used to maintain the position. Moreover, the legs are often under intense muscle contraction as opposed to a more relaxed state when performing the arched handstand. Hence, it is difficult to state which type of handstand requires the greatest expenditure of energy. The important factor would be more of a mechanical consideration than of energy.

The straight handstand enhances the downward swing by maximizing the effect of gravity through a longer lever. This factor would appear to lessen the internal force needed for an appropriate descent. Also, proper body alignment appears to reduce the energy requirement between the interaction of two or more skills. For example, moving from a handstand position into a pirouette is much easier when the body is straight than when it is arched.

Handspring—Cartwheel—Round Off

The forward flexing position of the hips positions the body so as to allow the hands to contact the mat. The body then rotates around the wrists as the axis of rotation. The forceful vertical lift derived from the arms and shoulders (during takeoff) is very critical to the success of the performance. The upward thrust should be as nearly perpendicular to the floor as possible. Less than 90 degrees lessens the vertical height of the center of gravity. The gymnast must compensate by bending the legs (which varies the moment of inertia to speed rotation) to land safely. The upward lift of the rear leg adds to the angular momentum already evident. It is this additional internal force that directs and positions the body through the desired path. The head (neck) is slightly hyperextended as the hands contact the mat. Visual cues facilitate proper muscular integration.

Hebbelinck and Borms (1968) state that the push-up phase from the floor results in a forceful interplay among a number of muscles. They determined by electromyographic action potentials the muscles most active at different phases of the front handspring. The projection phase utilized the: (1) deltoids; (2) trapezius; (3) triceps; (4) biceps; and (5) pectoralis majors. Collectively these muscles raised the center of gravity and increased rotational momentum. However, the biceps ceased to produce activity once the body began its postflight. This appears natural since the bicep muscle is a flexor muscle and the arm remains straight (due to the triceps). Yet, the biceps did participate in the push-up phase without flexion!

The cartwheel is utilized as a transitional skill to combine several skills into a common sequence. Hence, it is logically realized that the execution of the cartwheel results in either a positive or negative influence on the outcome of the subsequent skill. Regardless of whether the performer begins a cartwheel from a static position or upon consummating a prior skill, a force is necessary to either displace or continue displacement of the center of gravity from the base of support. With both conditions, the arms should be vertically placed above the shoulders. They serve to increase the lever arm. The hip flexion results in a faster descent. In addition, the leg lift and descent prior to bending at the waist transfers momentum from the legs to the body.

The bent push-off leg allows the hands to be placed close to the foot, followed immediately by its extension as the other (rear) leg reaches a near vertical position. Both factors increase angular motion.

As both hands support the body, the legs are straddled. This position is relatively easy since the center of gravity is lower than when the feet are together. At this point, visual cues are essential to maintain proper orientation. The head is not tucked or excessively raised, but is in more of a natural position for an inverted balance.

The hips turn a little to the side and continue piking to enhance the descent and contact with the mat. Both the pike and the push (action-reaction) by the hands increase angular momentum, which lifts the upper trunk to a vertical position.

Interesting variations of the two-hand cartwheel are the one-hand cartwheel and the aerial cartwheel (in which no hands are used for support). The basic difference between the two-hand and the one-hand cartwheel is the greater generation of angular momentum. This is accomplished by a more forceful: (1) downward motion of the one-arm, followed very quickly by a vigorous upward push; (2) pushing action from the floor by the bent leg; (3) upward-horizontal lift of the rear leg; and (4) descent of the first support leg.

The aerial cartwheel is performed without the support of the hands. Thus, the previously mentioned steps 2, 3, and 4 must be even more exaggerated for proper performance.

There are two basic differences between the cartwheel and the round-off. For example, both hands are placed side by side on the mat and the legs are straddled in the cartwheel. But, during the round-off, the hands are placed on the mat with a quarter turn, and the legs are together as the body assumes an inverted position. The gymnast turns about the long axis of the body to the opposite direction prior to the vigorous downward motion (hip flexion) of the legs.

The round-off converts forward linear momentum into backward angular momentum. An overly exaggerated forward-upward arm and leg thrust dissipates linear momentum (due to the pull of gravity) prior to its conversion into angular momentum. To fully use the forward momentum as a complementing impetus, e.g., for back handsprings, the performer should thrust his body forward-downward just before he initiates contact with the mat. He should not jump up into the air so to speak. The higher he jumps, the greater the loss of energy. So, stay low and convert the forces so as to enhance subsequent skills.

Front Somersault

The front flip is actually an exaggerated forward roll (Hay, 1973). The mechanics are essentially the same with both skills, yet differences do exist. For example, both skills are of rotational movement. During the front flip, the center of gravity acts as the axis from which the body rotates around. Yet, during the forward roll, the body also rotates around a point of support (the hands).

The time that it takes to perform both skills is highly dependent upon the radius of rotation and the summation of forces. Manipulation of these factors predisposes one to failure or success depending upon their application at the appropriate time. For example, upon completing the final phases of each skill, an extension of the body lengthens the radius of rotation, resulting in a decreased angular velocity for a more stable landing (Broer, 1973). An extension of the body prior to its appropriate lengthening response will often create difficulty in either landing (front flip) or in standing (forward roll.)

The front somersault is more subject to the force of gravity and its potential consequences than the forward roll. Hence, in view of this factor, the summation of forces (linear and takeoff) are critical to the success of the skill. The performer may, however, increase angular velocity to compensate for a poor directional application of force or a poor conversion of linear momentum to a vertical-horizontal, rotary motion by decreasing the radius of rotation via a modification in the tightness and duration of the tuck (Rasch and Burke, 1971).

By modifying the moment of inertia through a tighter tuck, the speed of rotation is increased (Tricker and Tricker, 1967). Likewise, a full extension of the body (layout position) decreases the speed of rotation (lengthening the radius of rotation). Upon realizing this relationship, an experienced gymnast can insure a successful completion of the front flip.

The takeoff should be as nearly vertical (90 degrees) as possible (Charteris, 1969; and Rasch and Burke, 1971). The more vertical the upward lift, the greater height the gymnast can attain to execute the necessary components of the skill. As the takeoff angle decreases from the desired 90 degrees, the interaction of the run (linear momentum) and the upward lift (angular momentum) materializes via a lower and longer (in distance) front somersault. This type of rotation is obviously not conducive to performance of subsequent skills due to a poor mechanical advantage.

The takeoff angle is influenced by the manner in which the arms are used in executing the front flip. Recently, the Russian method (arms extended rearward) and the traditional method (arms extended forward and overhead) of performing the front somersault have created considerable interest in determining the mechanical value inherent in each.

Fortier (1969) analyzed the reverse lift forward somersault and concluded basically that the Russian method was successful insofar as the basic components of the somersault were properly and efficiently integrated (timing and precision). He could not pinpoint one particular factor favoring this method except to say that the vigorous lift occurred as a result of a "coordinated effort between the leg-hip extension and the backward-upward drive of the rotated arms." Obviously this, too, is true of the traditional method when effectively executed.

However, Cooper (1968) presents evidence favoring the Russian method in terms of the vertical height attained and the speed of rotation of the front somersault. The performer was able to attain an additional upward thrust of 1½ inches when compared to the traditional method. Moreo·er, the reverse lift method favored more of a sitting position (hip and knee flexion) prior to takeoff. This factor increases the range over which force may be applied. It also places the extensor muscles on a stretch-response basis. Both conditions would tend to enhance the upward lift. Finally, in view of the principle of transfer of momentum from part to whole, the backward-upward velocity of the arms at takeoff was reported to be seven times the velocity of the arms when using the extended overhead method. This factor naturally facilitates rotational velocity, which helps to insure a more successful stabilization upon contacting the mats.

Double Backward Somersault

Without question, the double backward somersault is accomplished by a highly aggressive gymnast with the ambition to succeed in the performance of this skill. The tumbler needs all the linear momentum that he can acquire via the approach. Thus, the conversion of linear momentum into angular momentum (round-off into back handsprings) and finally into a vertical lift must be efficiently executed. In essence, the performer is in a position of adding force to accumulated force and the degree to which this is done dictates the outcome.

Pond and Ashmore (1966) state that the positioning of the feet may distract from the maximum lifting force. The feet appear important only to the extent that they relate to the positioning of the legs. Since the flips are supposed to be executed above the gymnast's standing height, the forceful extension of the legs must lift the body vertically. They also state that the first flip should be executed as the maximum elevation is reached.

The gymnast requires the necessary angular momentum to complete the flips by decreasing the hip and knee angles. Moreover, the head is hyperextended throughout the flips. Austin (1960) states that the second flip requires an even tighter tuck to insure complete rotation to the feet.

Upon landing, the knee angle increases more than the hip angle. That is, the performer is still leaning forward. However, this position is corrected as the performer's arms are raised above his shoulders and/or as the gymnast assumes a more extended position. Both conditions depend upon the type of skill that is to follow the double backward somersault.

PARALLEL BARS

Forward Half-Pirouette

This skill is learned first on the floor, low bars, then on the high P-bars (stationary and then by a swing). The support arm must be straight, the shoulder region must be extended, and the trunk and legs must be straight to reduce obstacles to the twisting action. A reversal of any of these factors creates learning problems. From a static position, the gymnast pushes off one bar with just enough force to move the center of gravity closer to the base of support. The head turns in the desired direction to enhance the total body twist (transfer of momentum from part to whole). Again, this principle is revealed as the released arm moves toward the bar. The arm may bend (although certainly not necessary) to hasten the regrasp on the second bar (shorten the radius of rotation of the arm). For a moment both arms come to rest on the one bar. The center of gravity is centered over the base of support. The weight is quickly changed to the second arm while the original support arm releases the bar and moves in the direction of the other bar. Upon regrasp, the gymnast must exert an internal force sufficient to keep the center of gravity within the base of support.

Reverse Half-Pirouette

This skill is similar in mechanics to the forward half-pirouette. However, it is generally more difficult to perform for several reasons:

1. The body moves backward to regrasp. This reduces visual perception to some extent.
2. A reverse grip is used instead of the overgrip. The latter appears to be a more stable grip.
3. Should the skill not be completed successfully, the performer usually experiences more anxiety about falling on his face, head, and shoulders since the turn places these segments between the bars. During the forward half-pirouette, however, the head position is outside (forward) of the bars.

Back Uprise Straddle-Cut Catch to a Handstand

The arms aid in the back uprise by forcefully extending and pushing against the bars (action-reaction). At the same time, the performer pikes to initiate forward progress of the legs. As the legs approach a near level forward position, the arms move quickly to the hip region to contact the bars. The regrasp of the bars permits a continuation of the original movement except in the reverse direction. As the legs descend underneath the bars, the arms bend and act as the axis of rotation. The body straightens as the legs move under the base of support. To compensate for this straight body position which must ascend against the pull of gravity, the shoulders move forward beyond the base of support. This adjustment, coupled with the bent-arm position, allows the center of gravity to remain close to the base of support (dynamic equilibrium), as well as reducing the resistance of the legs as they ascend. The pressing force is uniquely positioned to effectively lift the body vertically. The center of gravity is raised as the arms straighten. Balance is maintained as long as the resultant forces equal zero.

One-Arm Handstand

To maintain static balance in the one-arm position, muscular involvement is necessary to counteract the unstable movements inherent in the skill. As long as the outside force to upset static balance has been held at zero, the acceleration is also zero, resulting in a state of stable equilibrium.

The following techniques for maintaining static balance will help the gymnast to acquire the one-arm handstand:

1. The more obvious body positions used in the execution of this skill are: (a) the straddle-leg position; and (b) the legs together position. With the former, the legs are far apart as possible. This conscious movement of the legs denotes the first technique which is to decrease the height of the center of gravity. However, a one-arm handstand with the legs together is more difficult for several reasons: (a) the weight is directly above the supporting arm; (b) the center of gravity is much higher from the base resulting in a more delicate state of balance; and (c) the extension in the shoulder region is more difficult to keep due to the summation of forces directed downward.

2. It is important that the gymnast extend fully and constantly in the shoulder region upon the transfer from the two-arm support to the one-arm support position. The extended position of the shoulder will aid the transfer by keeping the center of gravity from moving outside the base of support. The hips should be slightly piked to counteract the tendency to pivot should the back arch.

3. The projection of a body part is of concern to the gymnast. Why? The arm not supporting the body acts as a lever to counteract the forces that tend to displace the center of gravity. For example, should a gymnast recognize movement too far to the right of the vertical line (center of gravity, shoulder, and hand), he may employ one or several methods of correcting the motion. He can drop the left arm and the body may move to the left. He can grip the bar more vigorously to help prevent further oscillation (side to side). He can forcefully contract the quadriceps and hip flexors (isometric contractions) to oppose the forces eliciting the faulty learn. Moreover, a movement of the right leg downward (in the direction of the fall) often aids in dissipating forces to the right due to an equal and opposite angular momentum taken up by the performer, whose position is thereby restored.

Stutzkehre

A gymnast usually begins the swing from the handstand position (static balance). The center of gravity is centered over the support. Appropriate muscular involvement produces the downward swing. The shoulders move forward past the hands to help keep the center of gravity close to the base. The descent is also influenced by gravity. This, too, must be controlled via internal forces.

As the legs approach the bottom of the swing, the shoulders are directly above the base of support. Again, however, the shoulders move beyond the perpendicular position. This time they move backward to compensate for the up swing of the legs. This type of a swing is generally referred to as dynamic equilibrium. That is, the center of gravity is constantly manipulated in a way that maintains balance.

The gymnast's hip region assumes a pike as the legs move upward. The piked position increases linear and angular momentum. The increased momentum reduces the resistance to the twisting phase of the skill.

One hand, e.g., the right hand, releases its grip just as the body reaches maximum height with the two-arm support swing. A forceful lift of the body through a gradual twisting motion is accompanied by the released hand. The velocity at which the released arm moves is faster than the total twisting velocity. Since the left hand is still in contact with the bar, the movement of the right arm across the body facilitates the twist (transfer of momentum from part to whole). The turning of the head, to the left, also reduces resistance to the twist. However, the most significant factor that seems to facilitate the twist (one-half turn) is the slight pike attained during the up swing. The pike shortens the radius of rotation, allowing the gymnast's body to accelerate. The increased momentum coupled with the other factors discussed help the gymnast to complete the one-half twist.

The support arm must remain in contact with the bar as long as possible to insure the desired alignment of the body. The legs should be nearly vertical when the support arm becomes airborne. The final push and the forward lean of the shoulder serve to provide an additional upward force. Maximum height is attained as the gymnast is airborne. As vertical progress finally reaches zero, the gymnast starts his return to the bars. The movement of the hands must be very quick to insure an adequate control of the downward forces. However, the gymnast may, in some cases, not go upward as much as he travels horizontally. In view of this, the summation and control of forces may be very great upon regrasp.

Bending the arm or leaning backward too much distracts drastically from the proper execution of this skill. In fact, even upon regrasp, the arms should not bend. Sometimes they do bend to absorb force or to disssipate too much angular momentum. It is best, however, that the arms remain straight and allow the shoulders to control forces. Balance is again obtained as the center of gravity moves within the base of support.

Diamidov

The obvious difference between the diamidov and the stutzkehre is that one hand (the support arm) remains in contact with the bars throughout the execution of the skill. Up to the point when the support arm becomes airborne during the stutz, both skills have similar body mechanics.

Whereas the stutz requires considerable linear and angular momentum to compensate for the moment when no force is being applied, the diamidov generally utilizes a less vigorous up swing. In fact, the up swing is highly controlled in preparation for the full twist.

The gymnast must initiate the twisting action during the up swing. The hips pike to enhance the movement of the legs upward. Hip flexion also aids the twisting action. The first half of the twist is complete near the inverted position. The released arm then moves in front of the body. The head continues its turn from the visually active position (down the support arm) to the next bar. The released arm flexes at the elbow. Thus, by shortening the radius of rotation of a limb, the limb moves with greater velocity. The final one-half twist is completed vertically. The flexed arm assumes an extended position prior to its contact with the bar. Both hands must secure the body by a very forceful grip. The arms must remain straight, shoulders extended, and no arch in the back. Hence, a straight handstand is the finished product.

Peach Basket—Handstand to Handstand

This information was derived from a cinematographical analysis of this skill as performed on the parallel bars. It was concluded from the study that the generally accepted coaching hints concerning this skill were for the most part valid (Boone, 1971).

Handstand-Descent

The main coaching points and results are:

1. The center of gravity must be within the base of support, the hands, for static balance.

2. The first noticeable movement was the legs. This was necessary to displace the center of gravity outside the base.

3. More energy was required to upset static balance than to just move the legs above the trunk. However, the energy requirement increased again to enhance the descent.

4. As the hips moved beyond the base, linear acceleration greatly increased.

5. Cervical hyperextension (raising the head) apparently helped to induce the descent action.

Swing

1. The swing involved a gradual decrease of the angle between the arms and the chest. The shoulders acted as the axis of rotation.

2. A gradual change in head position back to a more natural position was evident as the swing was more influenced by gravity and internal forces.

3. Centrifugal force was greater as the descent was more realized. It varied in relation to the muscular control of the descent.

4. The forward lean of the shoulders was necessary to maintain dynamic equilibrium. The lean counteracted centrifugal force and increased stability by moving the center of gravity closer to the base of support.

5. Prior to the pike (or entry between the bars), the gymnast almost stopped the descent phase of the skill. Apparently, this was in an effort to better control the swing. As the legs descended below the bars, they accelerated once again. Linear velocity of the legs increased some six times the velocity upon approaching the bars. Linear acceleration of the legs decreased as they approached the bars in front. This seemed only natural since the direction of movement was about to change.

6. Linear acceleration increased to its maximum (during the descent swing phase) during the time the legs were under the base of support (the performer's straight-arm support position).

7. The head moved forward (cervical flexion) as the legs swung above the bars. This was necessary to keep the body in balance.

Drop-Pike

1. Centrifugal force greatly increased as the gymnast initiated the drop-pike phase. Linear and angular acceleration increased, too, until the legs again changed their direction (downward to upward).

2. The hip angle decreased to enhance angular velocity.

3. Cervical flexion was less acute during this phase than during the prerequisite swing for the drop-pike phase.

4. Again, linear and angular acceleration reached maximum just under and in front of the base of support.

Extension

1. Hip extension reversed the direction of movement (for the third time). Hence, linear and angular acceleration were reversed (slowed).

2. Less energy was expended during the extension phase than during the drop-pike phase. This would seem correct, since the gymnast must expend a great amount of energy to just hang on to the bars to counteract the forces developed through the movement up to this point.

3. An effective utilization of the summated forces was possible as long as the gymnast maintained contact with the bars, however, as the grip lessened in intensity, less energy was used in controlling the body.

4. The arms stayed straight throughout the drop-pike-extension phase.

5. A specific point was reached in which the gymnast applied more force to enhance the vertical progress. This occurred just as the gymnast began his vigorous hip extension phase. Again, this was to be expected.

6. By thrusting the legs upward as vertically as possible at the end of the piked

pendulum swing, the gymnast increased the vertical lift. This emphasizes the importance of transfer of momentum from a limb (part) to the body (whole). The hands must be in contact with the bars (the base) to realize the effect of the extension phase.

7. The head was still positioned anteriorly. This action enhanced the vertical progress by reducing further, possible angular motion.

Release

1. During this phase of the skill, the gymnast's hands were not in contact with the bars. The gymnast could not alter the upward movement. That is, he could not gain additional height.

2. The summation of external and internal forces served to lift the gymnast above the bars.

3. Linear and angular acceleration and centrifugal force continued to decrease until no motion was evident. The gymnast reached a state of equilibrium in which all forces acting on the body were zero.

Regrasp-Press

1. The first movement was the positioning of the arms and hands for regrasp purposes. The gymnast's body position did not change during this time period.

2. The gymnast's head was in a hyperextended position. This seemed to enhance visual relocation and stability.

3. The internal forces (arms, shoulders, and back muscles) kept the center of gravity within the base of support. The arms were extended and the gymnast was in the handstand position once again, some 5.41 seconds later.

Recently, there has been some concern as to which method, the early or the late drop, yields the best results. The aforementioned analysis was based on a late drop. Lascari (1971) concluded that the late drop was not as effective as the early drop. The early drop resulted in a greater vertical impulse (force x time). Moreover, the early drop facilitated hip flexion and extension resulting in a rapid vertical force. He indicated that the results should be examined with some caution relative to negating the potential beneficial aspects of the late drop. In the author's opinion, this is a case in point in which unique individual differences must prevail. In the final analysis, both the early and the late drop require a secured and maintained grip to effectively transfer the summation of forces so generated to be realized in the extension phase above the bars. For the interested coach, Lascari also introduced a method for learning the felge. There are some interesting points and they may prove to be useful.

HORIZONTAL BAR

Kip

A gymnast overcomes inertia by flexing at the hips and arms. Then the legs are thrust up and forward. All of this is brought about by internal forces coupled with the principle of transfer of momentum. The overgrip is used in execution of this skill and it acts as the axis of rotation.

A gymnast may swing back and forth several times in preparation for the final forward swing from which the upstart is initiated. Upon a full forward extension of the body, the back may arch slightly. This is not necessary for a successful performance. However, the arched position does place the hip flexors on stretch and may result in a more vigorous hip flexion.

Harris (1939) states that upon finalizing the forward swing, the center of gravity remains parallel to the floor as the hips are flexed and the feet approach the bar. The center of gravity then follows a more vertical direction as the gymnast's hip extension places him above the bar. In that regard, Bunn (1955) states that the arms aid in directing the center of gravity. This is done by a forceful depression of the arms on the bar upon hip extension. As a result, the gymnast's body is moved closer to the bar and in a vertical direction.

Hip flexion at the end of the front swing prepares the gymnast for the force needed to overcome the pull of gravity. By flexing at the hips and securing an adequate back swing to the bar, the gymnast will experience an increase in angular momentum. As a result, the gymnast's center of gravity will move closer to the bar as the hips are extended. The finished product entails a support position above the bar.

Overgrip—Reverse Grip Giant Swings

Giant swings are basic to high bar work, particularly the overgrip and the reverse grip giant swings. Both types of swings utilize similar mechanics. That is, the center of gravity must be moved outside of the base to start the movement either forward (reverse grip, giant swing) or backward (overgrip, giant swing) of the bar. The body is stretched (lengthened) during the first quadrant of both giant swings to maximize the effect of gravity on the downward swing. Hence, the downward movement is accelerated. The body is shortened (piked) on the up swing during the fourth quadrant of both giant swings to minimize the effect of gravity, which tends to decelerate the up swing. In addition, decreasing the angle between the arm and the chest moves the center of gravity closer to the bar. This results in a shortening of the radius of rotation. Once again, the movement is accelerated. The increased angular velocity aids in positioning the center of gravity above the bar in a momentary handstand position.

Herrmann (1968) used a high-speed camera to analyze the overgrip giant swing. It took the performer 1.5 seconds to complete the swing from handstand to handstand position above the bar. Approximately 0.8 seconds of the total 1.5 seconds were used to descend beneath the bar. Up to this point, the performer continued to arch his back from 195 degrees to around 210 degrees. Actually, the hyperextended position is not as desirable as one might think. In fact, the arch distracts from the fully extended position discussed earlier in reference to maximizing the effect of gravity. The remaining 0.7 seconds were used for the up swing. Hence, according to his data, the performer completed the second 180 degrees (up swing) faster than he completed the downward swing.

According to Bunn (1955), data on an overgrip giant swing revealed that the performer attained his maximum speed between 135 and 180 degrees of the second quadrant. Moreover, velocity (ft./sec.) of the downward swing increased as the performer approached the bottom of the swing, at which time the up swing continued to decelerate as the performer assumed the starting position again. In this regard, gymnasts may exercise an easy (and technically better) technique to increase the downward velocity in preparation for the up swing by simply moving the hands a little closer together. If a gymnast, e.g., executes giants with the hands shoulder width or wider, the center of gravity moves closer to the bar, minimizing the effect of gravity on the body as it descends. Conversely, with the hands close together and the shoulders extended, the effect of gravity on the fully extended body will result in an increased angular velocity. The increased speed of rotation coupled with the correct body mechanics of the up swing will result in a realistic confrontation with the skill.

Free Hip Circle

This skill often follows an overgrip giant swing. Accordingly, this skill begins from an inverted position above the bar. There are two very obvious overt movements ascribed to the free hip circle. For example, the gymnast must descend to and around the bar. Second, he must rise above the bar in such a way as to aid subsequent skills.

Upon analyzing these two basic points more closely, one then can see the inherent difficulty in a commonly accepted intermediate skill. The performer, e.g., must descend to the bar, but not actually touch the bar. The descent is characteristic of dynamic balance in that the performer's shoulders move forward of the bar to draw the center of gravity closer to the base of support. However, a point (distance) is reached in which the center of gravity passes behind the bar and eventually outside of the performer's body as he initiates hip flexion to encircle the bar. Naturally, as the performer rotates from the forward position to a backward position, his descent increases. The velocity of this movement conjoined with the accelerated angular velocity (noted upon hip flexion) predisposes one to a bottoming effect, which often dictates the outcome of the performance. The feeling that one is about to be pulled off the bar is made worse should the gymnast quickly hyperextend the head. The additional transfer of momentum from the head to the body serves to complicate the desired confrontation with the summation of forces acquired up to that point. Hence, the head should be in a rather flexed position to counteract the effect of centrifugal force. The head is, of course, less flexed as the gymnast assumes a momentary handstand upon consummating the skill. The handstand is preceded by a gradual slowing of the movement as the gymnast fully extends his body during the up swing.

Cast to a Vault Catch

This skill requires a mixed grip. For example, usually the right hand is an overgrip and the left hand is an undergrip (reverse). To overcome inertia (Newton's First Law of Motion), an internal force (muscle contraction) is prerequisite. This is visually realized as the arms bend during the backward vertical progress. The shortening of the radius of rotation of a limb facilitates its speed of movement. At the peak of the back swing, the performer extends the body (hip and arm extension) as far as possible to obtain the highest forward vertical lift as one can to enhance the backswing beneath the bar. The fully extended body increases the downward descent to assist other forces in dealing with the pull of gravity realized during the final up swing. As the performer passes beneath the bar, the hips assume a slight to more acute (90 degrees) pike to increase angular velocity and reduce the effect of gravity that would exist with an extended body.

The forceful depression of the arms against the bar lifts the body vertically and eventually results in the desired horizontal movement necessary to complete the skill. In this regard, as the hips move close to the bar, the reverse grip releases as the arm positions itself for regrasp purposes. The overgrip is used as the last means of exerting force into the lift-and-pull action (Newton's Third Law of Motion). Both arms control descent by absorbing the force through a bent-arm position followed immediately by a straight-arm position.

The head always turns in the direction of the vault. An important point, however, is that the arms serve to aid in the twisting action too. After having passed over the bar and upon descent, the twisting action is aided particulary by the forceful extension of the arm nearer to the bar. Then, the shouders, hips, and legs complete the twist in that order.

Full-Turn Catch

The gymnast will usually extend the body on the downward swing to maximize the effects of gravity. Maximum acceleration is attained as the gymnast assumes a slight pike under the bar. The pike increases the available forces to overcome or, at least, minimize the effects of gravity during the up swing. The center of gravity moves first away from the base of support and then closer to the base as one hand is released to start the twisting motion. Since twisting movements are based on the transfer of momentum from part to whole and the longer and/or heavier the part initiating transfer of momentum the greater will be the twisting motion, the release arm should be extended first and flexed later. Finally, however, the bent-arm position does facilitate the movement of the arm by shortening the radius.

The turning of the head in the direction of the twist enhances the twisting motion. Such positioning of the head also insures adequate visual contact with the bar for regrasp purposes. Moreover, the twist is also aided by the downward and backward direction of force attained via the nonreleased arm. On the other hand, the support arm allows the body to continue its vertical process via the downward bending of the bar. This is based on the law of counterforce in which the applied force is not dissipated, but stored. Upon release of the bar, the performer's arm should bend at the elbow and prepare for the reach and regrasp of the bar. Flexion of the elbow and arm proper reduces the resistance to a change in motion.

The gymnast will reach a point vertically in which velocity is zero, at which time, the gymnast's descent will begin to take on additional speed (accelerate). As the arms come nearer to the bar, they will extend, slowing their motion. As a result, the regrasp phase should be a little easier, with increased chances of continuing the exercise.

Elgrip (Eagle) Giant

The mechanics of the eagle giant are essentially the same as discussed earlier in reference to reverse giants. The only obvious difference is that the eagle giant requires an inward rotated grip. The reverse giant uses a reverse grip. However, besides this point, the eagle giant is performed by a gymnast well trained in the basic giants as well as one who has developed a high degree of shoulder suppleness.

A gymnast may initiate an eagle giant by a stoop-in out of a reverse giant. There are many other possibilities as well. The lift of the body (vertical extension) in adjunct with the horizontal movement is made possible via the dislocation of the shoulders. The eagle giant is a dislocated giant swing. Hence, the more flexible the shoulders are upon descent and ascent, the less difficult it is to perform this skill.

Once again, it is necessary to fully extend the body during the downward movement and pike during the up swing. These movements maximize and minimize the effects of gravity. The up swing is made more stable as the center of gravity moves toward the grip (base support). The head should be hyperextended as one passes over the bar, at which time the body is extended, and the head assumes a more flexed (anterior) position.

Czech (German) Giant

The back kip is the ideal skill for lead-up purposes for the Czech giant. The kip places the gymnast in an arched position on the bar. Not to break the continuity of motion, the vertical lift of the body must be very quick. In one respect, the arched position is desirable in that it increases the distance through which the legs must travel. As a result, the legs develop considerably more momentum than the shoulders, which are more static at this time. In addition, an action and reaction effect may also evolve from the action of the legs pressing on the bar (law of action-reaction). The bar bends, stores energy, and releases it through the body.

The hips assume a slight to more acute pike above the bar. The downward press of the arms against the bar is very intense to sustain the degree of lift necessary for total commitment to the skill. The piked position reduces the moment of inertia (resistance); consequently, angular velocity increases as this force is applied sequentially with the downward force of the arms in opposite direction of movement.

The downward swing is characterized by a full body extension with exception of the shoulder arrangement. It is clear that at this time the gymnast needs to command all the forces possible to eventually finalize the motion at the top of the up swing. As the gymnast approaches the bottom of the swing, the hips begin to pike once again to shorten the radius of rotation—the end result being an increase in angular velocity. The gymnast must endure this phase of the swing. He should consciously make an effort to lead the up swing with the feet so as to avoid losing the appropriate shoulder angle. The final conspicuous piking of the hips at the top of the bar is essential for successful continuation of the swing.

Russian Giant

This skill, too, employs similar mechanics as discussed with the other types of giant swings. In this case, a gymnast may utilize a stoop-in as mentioned with the eagle giant progression. The Russian giant swing requires a reverse grip as the reverse giant does. However, the gymnast is able to see the bar as he passes over it at the top of the up swing during the reverse giants. He is unable to see the bar at any time during the Russian giant swing. This factor certainly increases the risk and difficulty of this skill.

The gymnast extends the legs at the top of the vertical lift. This action serves two functions: (1) it transfers momentum from the legs to the body; and (2) it serves to lengthen the body position. The shoulder angle increases to almost 180 degrees depending on the flexibility of the gymnast. Suppleness aids the performer in the learning of this skill as well as most gymnastic skills.

The down swing serves to accelerate the gymnast in preparation for the critical up swing. The hips begin to pike and the shoulder angle decreases as the gymnast approaches the bottom of the swing. These adjustments serve to increase angular velocity. In addition, the center of gravity moves closer to the base of support to increase stability. In this regard, a rather dramatic piking of the hips is noted during the up swing. This technique serves to conserve momentum.

As the gymnast approaches the bar, the hips continue their rotation to a point in which the hips are vertically placed above the shoulders. As the gymnast moves nearer the vertical position, entry into the next giant swing is facilitated by the vigorous extension of the body and an increase in the shoulder angle. Naturally, the head is flexed during the entire execution of the skill. Gymnasts cannot defer learning this skill if they are interested in national level gymnastics.

Endoshoot

From the handstand position on the bar, the gymnast very quickly and completely assumes a free straddle position encircling the bar and reaching the handstand again. This skill requires an undergrip or reverse grip and is sometimes referred to as an undergrip or reverse stalder.

The gymnast's shoulder angle decreases 90 degrees or less as the straddle position runs its course during the swing under the bar. In fact, the decreased shoulder angle probably plays the largest part in keeping the legs from unfolding (George, 1969). Nevertheless, the acute flexion of the hips does initiate the straddle-in position. Since the velocity of the movement is greatly increased by shortening the radius of rotation, the legs have a tendency to actually move downward (at the bottom of the swing) around the shoulders. Hence, suppleness is certainly a prerequisite for a smooth and desirable performance. The increased centrifugal force tends to pull the legs behind the shoulders. So, the acute hip flexion is not as consciously manipulated as it is specifically an outcome of correct mechanics.

The center of gravity moves away from the bar during the initial straddle-in, but it moves toward the base of support on the up swing. Again, the position of the shoulder on the up swing is characterized by a forward lean as the triceps move nearer the chest. Then, it becomes necessary for the angle to increase as the gymnast approaches the top of the up swing. The visual contact of the bar is an excellent feedback directing possibly some change in body position to insure success.

As the hands move onto the top of the bar for a more stable grip, the hips begin their rotation and vertical readjustment in which the hips are directly above the shoulders. The gymnast simply lifts the legs to the handstand position. The center of gravity is quickly placed outside of the base of support for continuation of subsequent skills.

Staldershoot

The straddle-in actually begins during the preceding giant swing. This type of action predisposes one to an accelerated entry into the down swing phase of the staldershoot or overgrip stalder. Furthermore, hip flexion places the legs past the bar before the shoulders reach such a position. The shoulders are, in fact, in front of the bar as the perfomer lowers to a straddle "L" support. As the hips are pushed backward away from the bar, the center of gravity moves away from the bar. Angular velocity greatly increases as the hips move beneath the base of support. Appropriate hip position and angular momentum is maintained via the decreased shoulder angle between the triceps and the chest. In fact, centrifugal force is greatest beneath the base. To counteract this force, the gymnast must keep a secure grip. At this time, the position of the head is basically flexed. To hyperextend the head would create additional angular momentum which often alters the desired flight.

The extension (straddle-out) of the body is accompanied by an increase in hip and shoulder angles. As a result, the up swing decelerates. At this time, the head position generally changes to more of an extended position to aid the continuation of the upward-horizontal movement. The gymnast assumes a handstand position for subsequent skills to materialize. The center of gravity must move outside of the base for continuation of the routine.

RINGS

Swing—Dislocate—Streuli

When performing on the rings, the center of gravity moves forward, backward, up and down. Again, as generally is always the case, the gymnast consciously manipulates the appropriate muscles to displace the center of gravity outside of the base of support.

A gymnast may initiate a swing by flexing the arms and lifting the legs, followed immediately by a quick and vigorous full body extension forward. Hence, the center of gravity is raised and moved from beneath the base of support (the hands and/or rings). The full body extension serves to develop sufficient momentum during the down swing to aid in the pendulum action of the body as it moves behind the rings. From this position, the forward swing culminates in reversal of motion for the execution of the dislocate phase of the sequence.

The dislocate begins with the piking of the hips and the movement of the center of gravity toward the rings. Obviously, the flexion phase increases angular velocity as is necessary for the subsequent semivertical lift of the body. The arms rotate laterally in adjunct with the shoulder adjustment (dislocation is misleading). If the chest is too low as one brings the arms forward, the pressure on the shoulder proper can be very intense. This is the reason for positioning the chest at approximately the same height as the rings. The movement of the center of gravity away from the rings denotes basically the completion of the dislocate—the final result being that the body is positioned so as to facilitate entry into the subsequent skill, the streuli. Thus, the execution of the streuli is highly dependent upon the effectiveness of the dislocate.

The initiation of the streuli actually begins as the gymnast's body descends from the dislocated position with the arms forward and the body position equal to or above the rings. The higher the dislocate, the greater distance through which the gymnast gains angular momentum.

As the hips pass beneath the rings, they begin to pike. By rearrangement of the body parts, the gymnast is able to reduce the resistance to motion. Moreover, he can effectively generate the desired velocity to aid in the vertical thrust of the legs, hips, and finally the chest and shoulders. Since acceleration is related to the force causing it, the flexion of the arms during the upward thrust of the body serves to complement the summation of forces realized at that moment. It has been fashionable for gymnasts not to flex their arms, but instead execute this skill with the arms straight. Naturally, this particular manipulation of the arms increases the difficulty of the performance. Nevertheless, the basic principles are the same.

A straight-arm streuli requires that the performer lift the shoulders well up into the rings during the upward thrust. This technique is technically more acceptable than the bent-arm position. At any rate, both techniques experience deceleration during the up swing until finally velocity is zero. That is, the gymnast is in a static position with the center of gravity within the base of support. Because this position is rather a critical one to maintain, the FIG Code of Points has designated that the hold position must be for a duration of two seconds (except the "L" support). The gymnast is now able to execute subsequent skills such as a giant swing backward or forward.

Giant Swing Backward—Forward

This skill begins from a handstand in the rings. One very important principle relative to the law of inertia is the continuity of motion. The execution of the down and forward swing must be smooth and without hesitation upon entering the upward swing to the handstand position. If the gymnast does, in fact, hesitate or pause during any segment of the entire giant swing, the apparent lack of poorly applied forces disrupts the technically correct continuity of the movement (skill). This principle applies to the giant swing forward too.

The giant swing backward begins with a backward movement of the legs while the shoulders move in front of the rings. The readjustment of the shoulder position keeps the center of gravity as close as possible to the base of support. This technique is necessary for maintaining dynamic equilibrium. The arms remain straight throughout the performance. Should the arms bend as the body descends, the effects of gravity will not be maximum since the length of the arm is shorter. Bending the arms also tends to dissipate the generation of forces. Once again, these basic mechanics apply to the forward descent of the giant swing forward.

However, the giant swing forward differs from the giant swing backward in one basic way. For example, the upward swing of the giant swing backward is enhanced and actually made possible by both hip and shoulder flexion (these adjustments reduce the resistance to motion and result in an increased angular velocity); whereas, the uprise of the giant swing forward is executed with shoulder flexion and a straight body.

Since the hips do not bend during the uprise of the giant swing forward, it would appear that this skill would definitely be harder to perform than the giant swing backward. The principle of conservation of momentum in swinging type movements supports the apparent difficulty. A gymnast shortens the radius of rotation to conserve angular momentum during the up swing. If a gymnast does not shorten the radius of rotation, he would fail to conserve momentum. The gymnast compensates with the shoulder lean which moves the center of gravity closer to the base of support. As a result, the uprise becomes more stable as the center of weight falls within the base.

Press to a Handstand

The press is an integral part of a routine. There are various types of techniques for pressing from a static position to another static balance. The easiest press is the bent-arm-tuck-press, which allows the center of gravity to stay relatively close to the base of support. The tuck position aids in increasing angular velocity. Hence, the performer expends less energy positioning the body vertically over the base.

The bent-arm-pike-straight-leg-press also keeps the center of gravity low and within the base. It is a little harder than the first since the straight legs require additional expenditure of energy to maintain the lift. The piked position tends to slow angular rotation. As a result, more energy is used in positioning the body than in lifting the body vertically. In essence, the continual adjustment of the hips and arms to one of straight body with the arms straight requires considerable energy to maintain the press as well as to maintain dynamic equilibrium.

The bent-arm-straight-body-press is commonly used by advanced gymnasts. This press is harder than the first two because: (1) the body is in an extended position; and (2) a major downward pressure is supported very quickly by the arms. Hence, the desired angular velocity is more difficult to achieve. This results in a large expenditure of energy in just positioning the body for the press. Furthermore, the center of gravity moves away from the base as the arms are extended. This in itself makes the handstand position more precarious.

The straight-arm-and-leg-press is generally believed to be the most difficult press. One must realize that individual differences, e.g., flexibility and strength, do exist and would be reflected in such skills requiring such qualities. In fact, if a gymnast is deficient in hamstring flexibility, he would probably execute a straight body bent-arm press and not the straddle-out press (straight-straight). However, for those individuals who are deficient in shoulder strength, but have adequate flexibility, they could engage in the straight-straight press. The abduction of the legs (straddle-out away from the body) serves to reduce the intensity of the press. If the legs are kept together as the hips attain the vertical position over the shoulders, the press is harder to accomplish.

Some basic principles of utilizing force are: (1) the force should be applied in accordance with the desired direction or intended motion; (2) the force should be applied constantly without pause or hesitation; and (3) the most effective application of force is at right angles to the intended motion. These principles should be used accordingly with each type of press.

Cross

Hay (1973) states that a body at rest has neither linear nor rotary motion. Obviously, then, such a position is one of static balance. For example, a gymnast performing a cross on the rings is in a state of equilibrium. The forces (forces exerted on the hands, the weight of the gymnast, and the force of gravity) must be equalized (zero) by muscular contractions to sustain the body at rest or otherwise a downward displacement of the gymnast would be obvious. It is possible, too, that a vertical displacement would occur provided the downward force of the arms and hands exceed the weight of the gymnast and the pull of gravity. To maintain the ideal body alignment (in which the gymnast is straight), the downward press of each arm against the rings should be the same (Hay, 1973; and Charteris, 1969).

The success of the skill (cross) is related to the length of the arms (Charteris). He states that a gymnast with shorter arms, when compared to another gymnast with longer arms but similar body sizes, will expend less energy and have an edge over his opponent with longer arms. Why? The shorter the force or weight arm (each extended arm), the greater the work capacity (in this case, strength) of the muscles in each arm. The task is easier because the gymnast can exert more force to stabilize the body. For the gymnast with longer arms, he must engage in a strength development program so that he may fully exploit his strength capacity since he certainly cannot reduce the length of his arms. The false grip is used to shorten the weight arm, but this technique is not as desirable as developing adequate strength.

Shorter arms also result in a closer positioning of the center of gravity to the fulcrum (the shoulder). This is supposed to lessen the intensity of muscle involvement, resulting in an easier performance. In reference to this particular point, Charteris points out that the "L" cross and the front lever are also difficult skills to perform correctly—the reason being that the center of gravity moves away from the fulcrum as the legs assume the "L" support and as the legs remain together during the front lever on the rings. In both instances, the center of gravity moves closer to the fulcrum if the legs are straddled during the lever and when the "L" support cross is changed to a cross. Likewise, this same principle applies to the handstand position. Spreading the legs lowers the center of gravity and makes the position more stable. However, as the legs come together, the center of gravity is raised, resulting in a greater possibility of upsetting balance.

SIDE HORSE

Double Rear Dismount

The feint position (on one pommel) is the beginning point from which the gymnast attains the necessary force and momentum for the movement. Provided the gymnast is supported by the right arm, the swing of the outside leg (right leg) over the end of the horse and the push of the left hand from the pommel generates the internal force resulting in motion. The right leg, in fact, completes 180 degrees and contacts the left leg prior to its movement in the desired direction. As the legs swing out over the end of the horse, the right arm supports the body. The hips flex to increase the speed of the movement and insure success. The right shoulder leans to the right to keep the center of gravity as close as possible to the base of support. As the legs swing forward and around the end of the horse, the left arm becomes the support. Again, as the legs pass over the pommel, the lean of the left shoulder is effective only if the arm remains straight. Thus, the left arm remains as the final support, keeping the body up and allowing proper transfer of momentum to finish the skill. The left hand remains in contact with the horse to aid in maintaining stability upon the descent of the legs.

Double Leg Circles—Tramlet

The double leg circle is as crucial to a side horse routine as legs are for walking. And, too, generally the beginner seeks to learn double leg circles as soon as possible, much as one must learn to walk before he can run.

A beginning point is usually a straddle position on the right pommel from which one leg (the forward, e.g., right leg) initiates a swing over the end of the horse to contact the rear leg (transfer of momentum from part to whole). From this point, both legs swing together to pass over the left pommel and eventually over the right pommel to complete one double leg circle. Once the gymnast acquires some experience with this technique, he may decide to start the swing from a standing position while facing the horse. Both methods employ similar mechanics.

The arms (or arm) must support the gymnast's weight. They must also control the center of gravity. This is accomplished by a lateral lean of the shoulder over the support arm. The grip must be secure and usually at the highest point of the pommel. The grip-release-push action must be quick and effective. It must also work in accordance with the shoulder lean to keep the shoulders over the pommels.

The movement of the legs is highly controlled by the action at the hips. As the right shoulder leans over the right pommel, e.g., the hips flex and rotate outward just enough to help extend the body as it passes over the left pommel. Hip extension during the front phase of the double leg circle is a very important step in learning this skill. As the legs move closer to the right pommel, the shoulders move laterally to occupy a position directly over the left pommel. The hips begin to pike as the legs pass over the right pommel. The hips are generally high in the back and extended in the front. Naturally, as the hips pike in the back, the velocity of the movement is enhanced in preparation for the front swing.

The head should remain in a natural position. An interesting point is that the head usually faces the direction of motion unless such a direction hinders the support of the skill. For example, as the gymnast's legs pass over the end of the horse, the gymnast may appear to be looking over the end of the horse. As the legs move in front and moreso upon passing again over the end of the horse, the eyes begin to look down the support arm as an aid in maintaining dynamic balance. This technique is more pronounced when one employs a tramlet (a travel).

The tramlet is a continuation of the double leg circle without a turn as in a kehre. As the gymnast's legs pass over the end of the horse to complete the double leg circle, the airborne hand is placed on the pommel already secured by the left hand. The left hand is placed on the back side of the pommel during the preparatory double leg circle. This position insures adequate room for the placement of the right hand. Both arms must remain straight to support the weight and force of the gymnast and the movement (law of action-reaction).

As the legs move from one end of the horse to the other end, the hips pike and raise the center of gravity as the velocity of the pendulum swing increases. Hence, the arms act as supports and the shoulders act as the axis of rotation. The right arm remains as the support arm. The lateral lean of the right shoulder draws the center of gravity closer to the base for increased stability. The legs continue the swing over the end of the horse. The left arm quickly moves to the end of the horse to support the continuation of the swing, e.g., as in a rear support with the legs circling over the pommels.

Moore (Czech)

This skill is almost always preceded and followed by double leg circles. The gymnast begins by a combination of a vigorous push of the, e.g., right hand from the pommel as the legs continue the swing with a gradual flexing of the hips. The right hand is placed on the left pommel in an undergrip position.

For a brief moment, the body is supported only by the left arm. As the gymnast's body assumes a quarter turn, both arms support the body. The initial hip flexion increases the velocity of the body as it approaches a more extended position over the end of the pommel. At this point, the gymnast's shoulders must be well over (or beyond) the support pommel. Naturally, this is necessary to increase stability. Dynamic equilibrium is maintained as the center of gravity is effectively manipulated via appropriate shoulder alterations. The arms must remain straight (action-reaction). And, as the legs pass over the end of the horse, the right shoulder accepts a major responsibility for supporting the body as it finishes the last half of the circle. The right shoulder must continue its movement to the right. The right arm must be straight while the left arm is raised and later lowered to quickly grasp the pommel for a more stable balance. The gymnast is now ready to execute, e.g., a double leg circle or a tramlet (traveling circles).

Doubles on the End (Loop)

A loop on the end of the horse may begin as a mount or it may follow a tramlet (downhill travel). Double leg circles on the end are not much different in mechanics than the regular double leg circles on the pommels. Both skills use a combination of forward, backward, and lateral leans.

Assuming that a gymnast moves from a tramlet into a double leg circle on the end, the support arm is the left arm. The arms must be straight. Moreover, they must be straight during the execution of all the skills on the side horse. The left shoulder must lean laterally while the hips flex upon passing from the pommel to the end of the horse. Again, shortening the radius of rotation increases the velocity of the movement. Since the gymnast is supported by one arm, hip flexion also moves the center of gravity closer to the base to increase stability.

Immediately, as the legs pass over the end of the horse, the right hand contacts the horse too. Both arms serve as the base of support. This position is generally easier, with less strain and uneasiness. However, as the body begins to turn and is supported by one arm (right) again, the execution of the skill becomes more difficult.

With both arms supporting the gymnast, the body is extended. The shoulders are in accordance with the side horse, but a forward lean is prevalent. The lean increases stability by keeping the center of gravity close to and over the base, the hands.

As the legs move forward, a pike is again evident for the reasons mentioned earlier. This time, however, the right arm supports the body. The right shoulder leans laterally. The lateral lean of the shoulders become less and finally it becomes more of a backward lean as the legs pass over the pommels. At this point, both arms support the body. The shoulders are definitely in back of the base of support. The hips are piked rather than extended as before in the two-arm support. The pike is necessary because the backward lean is not as far or as effective as the forward lean. Hence, the head is flexed to help prevent one from falling backward.

As the body descends around the horse and eventually to the end again, the shoulders lean first to the left and later forward. The main point is that the body (hips, shoulders, and head) assumes a position which helps to keep the center of gravity as near as possible to the base of support. Double leg circles on the end are often followed by a half twist loop dismount, moore without pommels, or an uphill travel (tramlet).

Stockli

This skill permits the gymnast to execute a reverse uphill travel into the saddle area (between the pommels) facing the opposite direction. Double leg circles may precede and follow the stockli. Thus, the stockli becomes a continuation of the first double leg circle.

To perform this skill, the gymnast must initiate and control two very important movements: (1) the lean of the shoulders; and (2) the positioning of the hips.

Upon completing a double leg circle, the left arm immediately begins to accept a major responsibility for the gymnast's weight. The arm must be straight (law of action-reaction). The shoulders lean forward as the hips pike (facilitating the movement of the legs). As the legs pass over the horse, the body is extended. The left shoulder must lean forward beyond the pommel to maintain dynamic balance.

The shoulders rotate in accordance with the swing of the legs and pass the horse. At this point, the left arm is not in a position to continue as the support arm. The center of gravity has moved outside the base of support, the one hand. Hence, the right arm must move exceedingly fast from the end of the horse past the left arm and pommel and on to the remaining pommel. The movement is enhanced as the arm bends at the elbow.

As both hands grasp the pommels, the shoulders lean forward to sustain the continuation of motion. The hips assume a pike as the swing is in alignment with the left pommel. As the legs reach the end of the horse, the left arm is raised to allow the passage of the legs. The support arm and right shoulder must lean laterally. Conversely, as the legs swing over the right pommel, the arm and shoulder lean laterally. The point is that the center of gravity must remain within or at least as near to the base as possible to sustain dynamic movement.

Magyar Travel

The performer must travel across the entire length of the horse in transverse posture. The legs must be kept above horse level—a factor which increases the difficulty.

Facing the horse with the left arm to the neck and the right hand on the horse, the performer begins with or from double leg circles in which the hands are rather close to the near or first pommel immediately to the right of the right hand. Upon grasping the first pommel, the arm is straight and the shoulder slightly beyond, laterally, to maintain dynamic balance. At this time, the body is fully extended and the hips are slightly in front of the neck of the horse. As the hips and legs move to a position in front of the pommel, the left hand must move to the first pommel too. The legs must remain straight, hips extended, arms slightly backward to the pommel, and chin on the chest. Each factor is crucial in maintaining balance.

As the performer's shoulders lean to the neck portion of the horse, the legs should be passing over the second pommel. This position is probably difficult to maintain in that the velocity is slowing. As the legs begin their descent and circular motion, the right arm again initiates the forward travel by moving to contact the horse between the pommels. It is very important to maintain a forward and lateral lean of the shoulders to aid in the continued motion of the hips and legs around the end of the horse. As the hips move between the pommels, the hands are not in contact with the pommels but instead the horse. Yet, as the legs continue their circular motion over the right or second pommel, the right hand moves to the second pommel and again similar events transpire as described when grasping the first pommel. The point is that the performer continues traveling by double leg circles by being first on, and then off, the first and then second pommel, until finally he reaches the opposite end of the horse, the croup (Urvari, 1973).

The most difficult part would appear to be the uphill travel from the saddle to the second pommel. Depending upon the performer's ability and skills, subsequent skills may entail a loop and dismount or whatever fits well with one's imagination and style.

VAULTING

Tsukahara

It is important that the performer reaches maximum linear velocity to achieve and expect an excellent postflight for the execution of the tuck or pike depending on the technique preferred. Upon contacting the horse, the hips and legs are generally lower than that of other vaults passing through the handstand position. The duration of the hands on the horse must be very short to prevent a major loss of forces. However, the 180 degree turn of the body through the longitudinal axis must be complete before the push-off is evident. Immediately after pushing off from the horse, the performer must quickly create backward angular momentum by raising the head and shoulders and by flexing the legs in under the body via a tuck.

It is necessary to exert an up and back movement of the shoulders and hips via the forceful downward push of the arms and shoulders against the horse with the counterforce being realized as the body approaches the desired height. It is of special importance, however, to realize that the push-off in and of itself is not sufficient to rotate the performer and make possible the following one and one-half backward salto. The necessary increase in angular momentum is derived from the leg snap (Wiemann, 1973).

Hecht Vault (Followed by a Forward Salto)

The approach run and takeoff are of vital importance to an excellent execution of this vault. The linear momentum and depression of the takeoff board must be sufficiently additive to create the necessary angular momentum to position the performer above the horse.

It is the purpose of the support phase to enhance the performer's flight. There are essentially two methods of contacting the horse, one being a downward push against the horse (which tends to create a backward rotation of the shoulders) and the other being more of a pulling action over the horse. The two methods of contacting the horse reflect the basic differences in afterflight of the handsprings and hecht vaults, respectively. The point is, however, that the performer must also do something else to achieve the desired afterflight and correct mechanics.

The performer is thus able to execute this skill by increasing his speed of turning around the transverse axis of the center of gravity by reducing his moment of inertia. This is brought about by tucking, which increases the angular speed of his forward turn. Yet, this is accomplished without a change in the angular momentum since the performer is basically a floating body upon becoming airborne.

The landing is made easier as the performer opens from the tuck and stretches for the floor, which correspondingly results in a decrease in angular velocity as the performer increases his moment of inertia (Wiemann, 1974).

Handspring (with 1/1 Turn Round the Longitudinal Axis)

On behalf of an excellent execution of this vault, the flight duration in the preflight, i.e. from leaving the board to contacting the horse with the hands, is influenced by the attained height. The longer flight time corresponds with the higher flight. It is reasonable to expect the preflight and afterflight times to be equal in duration, and thus they should be symmetrical.

The angle upon contacting the horse often depicts the angle at which the performer leaves the horse. The earlier the contact with the horse, the sooner the performer begins the afterflight phase (or, the larger the takeoff angle). Conversely, the later the performer contacts the horse, the smaller the takeoff angle, and consequently the landing is generally rough due to the lack of adequate flight time for proper adjustments. All of this, of course, is based on the time spent for the support. For the above comments to hold true, the push-off must be explosive and dynamic (with a time somewhere around .21 seconds from contacting and leaving the horse).

The afterflight phase can be adversely influenced should the preflight be too low just prior to contacting the horse. The performer is also forced to expend more energy in correcting the lower horizontal velocity derived from the low preflight phase. The performer may also land too close to the horse should the takeoff angle from the horse be too vertical. Hence, horizontal distance is reduced as the performer attains more vertical height. There must be a point, however, in which the takeoff angle would in fact favor an unsafe landing. This is readily realized when a performer extends too much vertically and not enough backward upon executing, e.g., a back handspring. The summation of forces is realized while fully extended, but without a sufficient backward thrust to allow the placement of the hands on the mat. The landing is indeed quite difficult and sometimes dangerous.

The performer must initiate the twisting action (360-degree turn) the moment the hands contact the horse to insure completion of the twist in time for landing. It should be remembered that the twist is possible (in this case) in the direction of the movement of the head and arm because the performer is still in contact with the horse. To initiate a twist otherwise without contact, the movement of the body would be in the opposite direction. However, the movement of the hips in the intended direction is often thought to be more significant than the use of the arms, which generally remain fairly extended above the shoulders and head (Bajin, 1973).

REFERENCES

Austin, Jeffrey M. "Cinematographical Analysis of the Double Backward Somersault," Urbana, M. S. Thesis, Univeristy of Illinois, 1960.

Bajin, Borislav. "Handspring with 1/1 Turn Round the Longitudinal Axis," *Olympic Gymnastics*. No. 4, (December, 1973).

Boone, Tommy. "A Cinematographical Analysis of the Peach Basket from Handstand to Handstand on the Parallel Bars," Unpublished Research Material, Florida State University, 1971.

Broer, Marion R. *Efficiency of Human Movement*. Philadelphia: W. B. Saunders Company, 1973.

Bunn, John W. *Scientific Principles of Coaching*. Englewood Cliffs, N. J.: Prentice-Hall, Inc., 1955.

Charteris, Jack. *This Is Gymnastics*. Champaign, Illinois: Stipes Publishing Co., 1969.

Cooper, J. M. "Kinesiology of High Jumping," Part 8 (Applied Biomechanics In Sports) *Biomechanics*, J. Wartenweiler, E. Jokl, and M. Hebbelinch (Ed.). Basel (Switzerland), S. Karger, 1968.

Cooper, John M., and Ruth B. Glassow. *Kinesiology*. Saint Louis: The C. V. Mosby Co., 1968.

Fortier III, Frank J. "Analysis of the Reverse Lift Forward Somersault," *The Modern Gymnast* Vol. 11, No. 12, (December, 1969), p. 14.

George, Gerald S. "A Second Look at Swing-Undergrip Stalder," *The Modern Gymnast* Vol. 11, No. 1, (January, 1969), pp. 20-21.

Harris, Ralph C. "A Cinematographical Study of the Upstart (Kip) on the High Horizontal Bar," Master's thesis, Springfield College, Springfield, Mass., 1939, in *The Modern Gymnast* Vol. 10, No. 3, (March 1968).

Hay, James G. *The Biomechanics of Sports Techniques.* Englewood Cliffs, N. J.: Prentice-Hall, Inc., 1973.

Hebbelinck, M., and J. Borms. "Cinematographic and Electromyographic Study of the front Handspring," Part 8 (Applied Biomechanics in Sports) *Biomechanics*, J. Wartenweiler, E. Jokl, and M. Hebbelinck (Ed.). Basel (Switzerland), S. Karger, 1968.

Herrmann, S. "Motion Recording of Gymnastic Exercises by Means of High-Speed Camera Shooting and Their Analysis," Part 8 (Applied Biomechanics In Sports), *Biomechanics*, J. Wartenweiler, E. Jokl, and M. Hebbelinck (Ed.). Basel (Switzerland), S. Karger, 1968.

Jensen, Clayne R., and Gordon W. Schultz. *Applied Kinesiology.* New York: McGraw-Hill Book Co., 1970.

Lascari, Arno. "The Felge Handstand: A Comparative Kinetic Analysis," *The Modern Gymnast* Vol. 13, No. 10 (October, 1971).

Logan, Gene A., and Wayne C. McKinney. *Kinesiology.* Dubuque, Iowa: Wm. C. Brown Company Publishers, 1970.

Pond, Charles P., and Jamile A. Ashmore. "The Double Backward Somersault," *Athletic Journal* Vol. 46, No. 6, (February, 1966).

Rasch, Philip J., and Roger K. Burke. *Kinesiology and Applied Anatomy.* Philadelphia: Lea and Febiger, 1971.

Scott, M. Gladys. *Analysis of Human Motion.* New York: Appleton-Century-Crofts, 1963.

Sylvia, Alfred J. "Advanced Skills for the Parallel Bars," *Athletic Journal* Vol. 48, No. 6, (February, 1968), p. 52

Tricker, R. A. R., and B. J. K. Tricker. *The Science of Movement.* New York: American Elsevier Publishing Co., Inc., 1967.

Urvari, Sandor. "The Magyar Travel," *Olympic Gymnastics.* No. 3, September, 1973.

Vega, Armado. "The Horizontal Bar," *Athletic Journal.* Vol. 51, No. 2, (October, 1970), pp. 42-45.

Wells, Katharine F. *Kinesiology.* Philadelphia: W. B. Saunders Co., 1971.

Wiemann, Klaus. "The Mechanical Effect of the Forward Leg Snap," *Olympic Gymnastics.* No. 2, June, 1973.

Wiemann, Klaus. "Hecht Vault, Followed by a Forward Somersault," *Olympic Gymnastics.* No. 3, September, 1974.

Index